Praise for Driving Force

Driving Force tells the inspiring story of how one patient took control of every aspect of her recovery and proved to us all that motivation and dedication may be the most important drivers of outcome after trauma. Paula Franetti's engagement in the recovery process is evident in every chapter and this is undoubtedly why she has surpassed all of our expectations.

Gele B. Moloney, M.D.
Orthopaedic Trauma Surgeon

Paula Franetti is an amazing and inspiring person. In *Driving Force*, she takes us on her challenging personal journey, recounting not just the hurdles brought on by the devastating automobile accident that almost claimed her life, but the personal and professional support she garnered in her rehabilitation that are key to human resilience. This book is a must-read for anyone who has, or is experiencing a setback, and for those who love someone in the clutches of a challenging situation.

Al Condeluci, Ph.D.
Former CEO Community Living and Support Services

Driving Force is a must-read for anyone who has undergone an injury with lasting effects, regardless of severity. Paula Franetti's recounting of her journey is a gift of understanding regarding the immense power of belief, hope, and positive thinking. Paula's journey from near death to a return to competitive athletics, all in her 60th year, is extraordinary. From the very beginning, she took charge of her mind as the primary modality toward wellness and beat all odds to make a full recovery from devastating injuries to her entire body. I don't know of a single person, who could not use this book as an inspiration. Its well-defined principles and practical tools are useful for overcoming obstacles of any kind.

Lori Wynn, PT, DPT
Lori Wynn Physical Therapy

Paula Franetti has always been a person of integrity and excellence. Her work on *Driving Force* is another representation of her skill, talent, and determination. She tells the story of her experience with honesty and vulnerability, creating a model for how to not only manage trauma, but heal from it, heart, mind, and body. If you ever have a healing challenge in your life, you'll want to keep *Driving Force* close by as an inspiration and a guide.

Nancy Mramor, Ph.D.
Award-winning Author, Health and Media Psychologist

Driving Force eloquently expresses the strategy required for successful health crisis recovery—purpose, organization, and adherence to a personalized plan. Paula Franetti's work is fresh, inspiring, and most of all, useful.

James Bauerle, Esq.

Wonderful message! This book is a brief journey into how one woman used the power of positivity to overcome all odds to return to her previous active lifestyle. A must-read for anyone facing a difficult challenge.

Sheila Miles, RN
Risk Manager
Patewood Rehabilitation and Healthcare

Driving Force is a riveting reminder of the power of the human spirit to fight for life and recovery. It is a tale full of power, vulnerability, and self-awareness we all can relate to. This approach uses our strengths and weaknesses to mold our own plan for spiritual recovery, a return to physical health, and peace."

Lynne E. Porter M.D., FACP

The mind/body/spirit concept in *Driving Force* supports the essence of Occupational Therapy. In addition, Paula Franetti provides an excellent insight into the compliance/noncompliance tension in the use of adaptive equipment. As an Occupational Therapist, I endorse Franetti's six principles as a critical part of any therapeutic intervention.

Tina Bruns, OTR/L

Driving Force is Paula Franetti's story of winning over a life-threatening injury. More importantly, it is a guide for patients in their recovery from catastrophic injury in all three facets: physically, emotionally and spiritually. As a nurse practitioner who works in orthopedics, I will highly recommend this book to patients, so they realize others who have been through the struggle and won. I will also recommend it to families, so they can gain insight into the experiences and feelings of their loved ones. Lastly, I will recommend this book to my colleagues as we professionals need to understand what our patients experience as well as help patients with the six principles Paula so capably describes. This book is a must-read.

Kathy Barton, CRNP

Ms. Franetti's book is an uplifting and necessary testimonial to the power and critical role of the human spirit to endure great physical injury and drive one's own recovery, often through seemingly insurmountable debilitation. As most healthcare professionals recognize in severe cases of trauma, triumph over illness may only be initiated by the powers of modern medicine and surgery—it is the desire and will of the patient that is often the key factor in completing the journey to a successful and positive outcome. Without this, our best efforts as healers may often fail. Ms. Franetti's experiences and insights serve as an inspiration to patients going through the process of recovery after traumatic injury and provide a personal roadmap to successful physical and spiritual rehabilitation in the face of significant physical adversity.

Inderpal (Netu) S. Sarkaria, MD, FACS
Vice Chairman, Clinical Affairs Director,
Thoracic Robotic Surgery
Co-Director, Esophageal and Lung Surgery Institute
Co-Director, Thoracic Quality and Outcomes
University of Pittsburgh Medical Center

DRIVING FORCE

How One Woman Rebounded from Life-Altering Injuries and You Can Too

Paula M. Franetti, MS, CHC, CPT

DRIVING FORCE

How One Woman Rebounded from Life-Altering Injuries and You Can Too

To contact Paula:

Website .... https://www.ReboundPlanner.com/
Email .... paula@ReboundPlanner.com
LinkedIn .... https://www.linkedin.com/in/paula-franetti/
Blog .... https://www.reboundplanner.com/blog/
Facebook ...... https://www.facebook.com/ReboundPlanner/
Twitter .... https://twitter.com/ReboundP

To contact the publisher, inCredible Messages Press, visit www.inCredibleMessages.com.

Printed in the United States of America
ISBN 978-1-7322510-4-5

Book Strategist & Editor ..... Bonnie Budzowski
Cover Design .... Bobbie Fox Fratangelo
Author Photographer.......... Anita Buzzy Prentiss

Dedication

To my sister, Nancy,

Ti voglio tanto bene, mia cara sorellina.

ACKNOWLEDGMENTS

THE URGE TO WRITE THIS BOOK began during the long, lonely months of healing and rehabilitation when I realized the responsibility for my becoming well was up to me. But it wasn't until I attended a book writing workshop by Bonnie Budzowski of inCredible Messages, that I knew my rebounding story could be of value to others. Without Bonnie's book coaching and her incredible knack for bringing out my best writing, this book would have remained a mere idea. I am grateful for all the encouragement, brainstorming sessions, and creative editing Bonnie and I shared to make this book a reality and blessing to all.

I am grateful to the UPMC Mercy trauma team that saved my life and provided exceptional care that enabled my body to heal. I am eternally grateful to: Garth A. Elias, M.D., attending general surgeon; Gele B. Moloney, M.D., orthopedic trauma surgeon;

Ronald M. Benoit, M.D., urology surgeon; the Emergency Trauma Center personnel; and the tremendous doctors and nursing staff in Trauma and Burn ICU. Your expertise and care gave me a solid foundation for healing.

A special thanks to Gele B. Moloney, M.D., who saw me throughout my rehabilitation. I truly appreciate your willingness to answer my many questions and the respect you showed in my pursuit of stretching beyond healing to becoming fully well.

Special thanks goes to these health practitioners who provided medical care for complications and/or rehabilitative guidance: Inderpal S. Sarkaria, M.D., UPMC thoracic surgeon, whose expertise enabled me to resume the cardiorespiratory lifestyle I desire; David O. Wilson, M.D., UPMC pulmonary specialist, who discovered my diaphragm complication; Dr. Suehun G. Ho, M.D., physical medicine and rehabilitation specialist, who listened and found the solutions I needed; Alicia H. Puskar, Psy.D., neuropsychologist at the UPMC concussion clinic, who provided encouragement and guidance; Nancy Mramor, Ph.D., psychotherapist, who enabled me to "delete" the effects of trauma; Kim Craft, RBP, for all the Bowen and muscular integration treatments; and Susan Petrella, M.Ac., whose acupuncture treatments finished my healing.

I thank all the witnesses and bystanders who helped in whatever way with pictures and information about the accident. Heartfelt thanks to Darlene Anderson and Jamie Creach for their heroic actions in getting me to safety and keeping me conscious.

A loving thanks to my devoted family members who stayed by my side throughout this long healing journey. I feel so blessed to have the family I have. I don't know what I would have done without your support. To my sister Nancy, who dropped everything to come when I needed her most and who continually stuck by me. To my brother, Jeff, who never gave up on me and did what he could to help me recover. To the stalwart supporter of our Gayarsky family, Patty Steinle, for being my hospital advocate and for all the help she provided. To Helen and Nick Samila, Dave Samila, and Bill Gregor, who stayed by my side in ICU. And to all my cousins who visited me, sent prayers, cards, flowers, and best wishes for a full recovery.

Extra heartfelt thanks go to Glenda Breth-Marcozzi who came from Italy to care for me for six weeks. I cannot express how grateful I am for all that you did and the sacrifices you made. You went through the roughest patches with me and ultimately taught me the dance of receiving help. A special thanks to Massimiliano (Max) Marcozzi, and children, Lavinia and Michelangelo, who graciously encouraged Glenda to be here for me.

No one can go through a recovery like this without the love of a dedicated tribe of supporters. I can't express how deeply grateful I am for all the different forms of love my tribe provided. Your countless visits, household tasks, rides, meals, legal advice, medical guidance, Bowen treatments, haircuts, help getting me in and out of my house, and most of all, your deep abiding friendship, made an enormous difference.

Special thanks to Trish Wood, "Schaack" (Laura) Schatzkamer, Susan Veraldi, Lisa Adamsky, Tina Bruns, OT, Nancy Graham, Kim Craft, RBP, Joanie Tutin, Liz Deemer, Esq., Dianne Wainwright, Esq., Lynne Porter, M.D., FACP, and Lori Wynn, DPT, for all the extras you did. And to my teammates from the Senior Olympic Butler Pursuit team; the Butler Cubs organization; Steel City Dragons team; and sister basketball team NOVA Triple Threat.

Lastly, the reason I have a story to tell is because of my faith in a Higher Power and the everlasting Laws of the Universe. May we all be open to discovering the life-giving meaning within any health circumstance we encounter.

Contents

1.

Was It a Miracle?

TODAY MARKS THE ONE-YEAR ANNIVERSARY of the automobile accident that almost killed me. People are convinced that my survival was a miracle; however, I'm not so convinced it is true.

I suppose that surviving a near-fatal accident does count as miraculous. Medical professionals tell me that my survival was questionable and that I beat the odds. And, yes, I did exceed everyone's expectations by fully recovering from my horrendous injuries.

Still, I question: Was my healing truly a miracle or was it something else? Did I do something that others may not have done in my situation?

I've decided to reenact the accident today to find answers to these questions. I am parked in my car a stone's throw away from the intersection where I was brutally blindsided. I plan to drive through the intersection at the exact time as I did one year ago today.

Through all the struggles I endured this year, I somehow healed beyond expectation and became fully well again. I hope that by reliving the circumstances of the accident I can become more certain of what made this possible. Was it a miracle? A fluke recovery? Or have I discovered a valuable healing process from which others facing tough recoveries can benefit?

Friends say it's a miracle I can walk again and live without chronic pain. Some also say, "Oh, but you were in such great shape before the accident," as though being fit guarantees a full recovery from an injury or illness. No, regaining my health and wellbeing wasn't a natural outcome kind of thing. It required quite a bit more than simply resting on my fitness laurels and waiting for wellness to show up.

I wonder if people assume my recovery was by default because I am a health professional. Being a health coach with a background in exercise physiology, movement biomechanics, and orthotics and prosthetics *did* give me an advantage. I could work cooperatively with my physical therapists (PT's) and perform exercises correctly on my own. Still, knowing what to do didn't magically make me walk again.

"Yeah, but you have such a positive attitude and that's what made you well," people say.

As far back as I can remember (and now to my chagrin), my mom called me "Pollyanna," a name I neither understood nor appreciated as a young child. I was well into my teens before I learned that Pollyanna could find something to be glad about in almost every circumstance she encountered.

While I was embarrassed to be described this way while growing up, I naturally did foster a positive attitude throughout my life. Why not look at the proverbial glass as half-full? Lots of research shows that a positive attitude leads to favorable outcomes in productivity, health, and wellbeing.

Trust me, though, I wasn't wearing rose-colored glasses as I digested the news of my extensive injuries. When I became coherent enough to understand the extent of my injuries (following the accident and multiple surgeries), I was as overwhelmed as anyone would be. I feared I had lost my professional livelihood and the active lifestyle I treasured so much.

And it wasn't until I was out of the skilled nursing facility and slowly regaining my strength and independence that more injuries and setbacks surfaced. The unceasing one-step-forward-and-three-steps-backward setbacks, especially the emotional trauma, were daunting.

So what actually caused me to fully recover and become well again?

Was it simply a miracle that God or karma or some astrological alignment bestowed on me? Can it be chalked up to luck that I got an exceptional medical team the day of the accident? And was it my doctors who made me well? Or did I create my recovery by wanting so much to be well?

I don't know for sure. There is one thing, however, of which I am certain:

During my recovery, I encountered mountain after mountain of push-me-to-my-limit challenges, which led me to discover certain principles that kept me believing I could get well. Was it this set of principles and the faith I placed in them that made me fully recover?

Getting through this intersection today will help make it clear.

I hesitate though. I'd be lying if I said I wasn't petrified to drive through the same intersection that created the horrid memories of what happened one year ago today.

Yet, I know that being able to reach the other side of the intersection will validate that the beliefs I developed and the actions I took to get well really do work. It will prove to me and others that following the principles I discovered is what enabled me to recover from the mental, emotional, and physical trauma of the accident.

8:33 A.M. The traffic light on Jumonville turns red.

Well, here goes, I think to myself.

Swallowing hard, I slowly pull out of my parking space to become the lead car at the traffic light. As seconds tick by and vehicles fly down Forbes Avenue, I breathe deeply, grip my steering wheel at ten and two o'clock…and wait.

8:35 A.M. The light turns green.

"Ready, Paula?" I say to myself. My heart is racing, beads of perspiration collect on my brow, and my grip tightens.

I look up Forbes Avenue. I look again. I look a third time before stepping on the gas pedal and moving forward to find my answer.

It is during our darkest moments that we must focus to see the light. ~Aristotle

2.
Blindsided

A **MILLISECOND OF SCREECHING TIRES**, then, *KABOOM*—my life changed forever.

Until that moment, I was enjoying a full and invigorating life, spreading my entrepreneurial wings with an online health coaching business in Pittsburgh, Pennsylvania. Having recently turned 60 years old, I was feeling in my prime and certain I had a long, healthy, active life ahead of me.

As luck would have it that particular morning, I got the dreadfully long red light one block from my shared working space in StartUptown. My standard commute followed the lightly trafficked Jumonville side street to cross Forbes Avenue, the main artery connecting downtown Pittsburgh with Oakland. At 8:35 a.m. on Tuesday, September 13, 2016, the light on Jumonville finally turned green and I mindlessly drove across Forbes.

Witnesses estimate the driver who hit me was exceeding 55 in a 25-mph zone when he ran the red light and rammed directly into my driver's side door, practically folding the car in half. The massive blow spun my car counterclockwise down Forbes, barely missing a traffic light pole and jumping the curb. My Honda's backend ricocheted off the front wall of the second rowhouse then bounced to a stop more than 30 feet past the collision site on Jumonville.

All I remember about that surreal moment is the unforgettable crushing sound of the car's impact and clenching the steering wheel as my body flung hard to the right.

What in the world hit me? The thought flashes through my mind, seconds before everything goes black.

Before an answer forms, the car settles and as if by magic, I feel just as I imagine Dorothy and Toto did when they landed in a place far from home.

Everything that was perfectly routine and familiar seconds before is changed, and I do not recognize where I am. The overcast, humid morning and the noise of Forbes Avenue are gone. In their place, I am in the countryside with clear blue skies and the warmth of the sun bearing down on me. Or is it some other kind of light shining on me? I cannot tell.

I find it strange that although I was driving my car, it is no longer here. The only remnants of my Honda CRV are the steering wheel I still hold and the driver's seat on which I am sitting. As bizarre as everything appears, I feel as safe and secure as a baby nestled in its mother's arms, oblivious to its surroundings.

It's so quiet, I think to myself, as though I am inside an invisible isolation booth designed to keep me from being distracted. Impulsively, I break the silence and announce to whoever is listening, "Where am I?" "What is happening…am I…, did I…." I say aloud, "I must have just died."

No one answers, and the silence continues. Strangely, asking aloud if I died releases a wave of indescribable peace and joy throughout me that I have never felt before. It washes away any need I have for answers, and I realize wherever I am and whatever is happening, it is very good. So much so, that I am certain I do not want to leave.

Then, as suddenly and unexpectedly as the impact happened, my incredible serenity vanishes.

Out of nowhere, deafening, chaotic voices and wildly-waving hands fly at me from all angles. I feel my body being slammed back into my car's interior, tied down by a seatbelt strangling my neck.

A crowd forms on the street, someone calls 911, and help is dispatched immediately. Darleen Anderson takes charge, a 58-year-old nurse who, by chance, lives two doors down from the house into which my car has plowed.

Having heard the impact, Darleen runs to my car, barefoot and in her nightgown, and discovers the life-threatening situation unfolding. A middle-aged woman is trapped inside a crushed, smoking automobile with leaking gasoline that can possibly burst into flames.

Without a concern for her own safety, Darlene goes into nurse mode and takes immediate steps to determine if I am alive, and if so, how badly I'm injured. She does a quick assessment and finds only minimal external bleeding and no obvious fractures. Darlene has no way of determining the extent of possible internal injuries, but she can see I am slipping into shock.

Making a lifesaving decision, she shouts, "We gotta get her out of the car!" More people assemble, including Jamie Creach, a painting contractor who, along with some of his crew, witnessed the accident.

With the help of Jamie and his crew, Darlene is able to slip inside the vehicle to try to disconnect the seatbelt and determine how to extract my body. It is not going to be easy though. The forceful impact has shoved the seat forward and diagonally into the console, leaving the seatbelt fully extended and slicing into my neck. Unable to release the jammed belt, Darlene runs to a neighbor's house for a knife to cut through it and release the pressure.

Once I am freed, Darlene and Jamie devise a plan to remove my body before the car ignites. Jamie volunteers to squeeze his body inside the cramped quarters. He puts his arms under my shoulders and, as gently as possible, lifts me through the passenger door.

Excruciating pain erupts from my back and pelvis, causing wails of agony that make me realize I cannot breathe properly. Feeling as though my lungs are unable to hold air, I begin to panic, which constricts my airway even more. I shudder, thinking that I am going to suffocate.

Somehow, I remain conscious, but now I'm genuinely afraid.

Jamie places my limp body into the locked arms of two of his crew members who carry me across the street to a concrete porch stoop and gingerly lay my back against Darlene's legs. Darlene, instinctively nurturing, does everything possible to keep me conscious while we wait for first responders.

Wheezing breaths, agonizing pain, and terrifying unknowns make me want to return to the peace and tranquility that were mine just short moments before. Desperate to end the pain and return to that state, I ask Darlene, "Am I dying?" I say this with a hint of, "Please confirm this is true so I may return to where I was!"

Darlene replies "No, no, you're not dying. Honey, you're going to the best trauma unit in Pittsburgh." In disappointment, I realize that I am going to remain in this world for now and face an unforeseeable future.

Emergency Medical Services (EMS), city firemen, and Pittsburgh police arrive one by one to size up the situation. The EMS professionals perform a rapid trauma assessment and suspect I have a lateral-shearing unstable pelvic injury with potential spinal cord damage and internal hemorrhaging from the Honda's forceful T-boning. Due to my decreasing blood pressure and the concern of severe internal bleeding, my status requires a high-priority transport. EMS personnel immediately stabilize my neck and pelvis and continue monitoring for shock.

Firefighters douse the car and sweep away debris from the street while police and witnesses piece together what happened. As soon as I am stable, the ambulance rushes me to UPMC Mercy Trauma Center, fortunately only four short blocks away.

Emergency medical providers know that decisions made within the first 60-minutes of a major trauma, the so-called *golden hour,* make the difference between life and death. The quicker intervention happens, the better the survival rate and recovery for the patient.

By the time I reach UPMC Mercy, only 38 minutes of my golden hour have expired.

UPMC MERCY TRAUMA CENTER

Trauma units, unlike emergency departments, specialize in life-threatening critical injuries where immediate survival is at stake. Little did I know how correct Darlene was that I was going to the best trauma center in the area.

UPMC Mercy Trauma Center is the only combined Level I Regional Resource Trauma and Comprehensive Burn Center in the Pittsburgh Tri-State region. Its state-of-the-art program staffs round-the-clock in-house attending trauma surgeons, surgical critical care physicians, and a full complement of highly trained nursing and technological personnel.

Within seconds of my entering the trauma center, systematic emergency medical procedures begin. Calm and caring introductions precede a blur of medical and administrative personnel speaking to me and about me with focused intent. The fact that I am conscious and somewhat able to communicate makes getting through age, birthdate, consents, medications, and allergies swift.

I notice actions are intentional and precise all around me. Emergency trauma personnel cut away my remaining clothing to make room for IV's, EKG leads, a blood pressure cuff, pulse oximeter, and blood draws.

At some point, an attendant assures me that my computer and phone are now with my belongings. Given that I am single and live alone, I figure I better let someone know about my accident since I have no idea what lies ahead. Flagging a nurse, I ask if she can make a few calls for me.

The first call is to my sister, Nancy, in St. Petersburg, Florida, to let her know I was in a horrific automobile accident. The second call is to my good friend and neighbor, Tricia Wood, whom I am supposed to pick up at the airport this evening. Knowing I will not be driving anywhere soon, I want Tricia to know she will need a new jitney driver.

A little after 9:25 a.m., and still within the critical golden hour, emergency trauma workers rush me to radiology to get a high-level assessment of my injuries. The findings lead to a detailed full-body CT scan of my head, spine, and pelvis to determine the specific extent of my injuries and determine the makeup of an intervention team.

The summary of the diagnostic reports reveals there is plenty to do that day.

A Force to Be Reckoned With

The EMS professionals at the scene had assessed correctly: The cumulative force of the lateral T-boning impact did indeed cause an unstable pelvic circle injury.

At impact, the side and steering wheel airbags deployed, intensifying the power that hurled my strapped-in body directly into the driver seat armrest. Twisting and shearing forces such as these literally wring the pelvis and abdominal region like a wet washrag, snapping bones in the anterior and posterior pelvis. The injury is classified "unstable" because the circular pelvic basin, which protects major blood vessels and lower abdominal organs, disrupts and takes on the shape of a twisted oval.

In my case, the front upper portion of the pelvic ring (called the superior ramus) shattered into pieces on the right side and caused a displaced fracture on the left. Both lower connecting bones (called the inferior rami) fractured on each side of the lower pelvis.

The back of the pelvis (sacrum) and each side of the pelvic basin (ilium) are connected by the strongest ligaments of the body, forming the sacroiliac (SI) joint. Thankfully, my ligaments stood their ground upon impact; however, the bones they connect to gave way. Just beyond the anchor point of the SI ligaments, two vertical fractures occurred at both borders of the sacrum and ilia. The most dangerous pelvic injury, however, was on the right side of my sacrum. It snapped like a pretzel through the holes where the sciatic nerve roots exit.

The rapid twisting of jagged and disarranged pelvic bones punctured my bladder and tore blood vessels, producing active bleeding in the posterior pelvic cavity. The wringing action also snapped four lumbar transverse processes, which are the small bony projections off the right and left side of each vertebra.

Rarely do unstable pelvic injuries from lateral impacts occur in isolation. Statistics show lateral impacts are three times more likely to cause a resulting diaphragmatic rupture. A typical tear from an auto accident measures 5-15 cm, usually on the lateral backside of the diaphragm. My tear was 8 cm, large enough for my proximal stomach and spleen to push up into the chest, encroaching my heart. The blow collapsed the lower lobe of my left lung, creating a small air pocket and adding to my distressed breathing. The right lung, somehow, escaped injury.

Mercifully, the force of the impact spared my ribs but landed hard on my neck. The unanticipated lateral hit whiplashed my neck and head like a ragdoll in a dog's mouth. My brain was bobbled side-to-side, then front-to-back, when the car was hit and when its backend bounced off the rowhouse. It's hard to measure the amount of soft tissue damage my upper neck sustained. We know that at least the C7 transverse process fractured and I sustained a mild concussion, fortunately without a bleed.

PUTTING HUMPTY DUMPTY TOGETHER AGAIN

At 10:43 a.m. the emergency trauma team completes its advanced trauma life support protocol and establishes a risk-stratified plan to treat my diagnosed injuries. In total, my body sustained seven pelvic fractures, five transverse process fractures, internal pelvic hemorrhaging, traumatic bladder and diaphragm injuries, and a mild concussion. Non-life threatening injuries—cuts, bruises, and soft tissue injuries—were noted and would be addressed once the life-threatening injuries were addressed.

My treatment begins with the injury deemed the highest priority–the hemorrhaging in my pelvis. In addition to the pooling blood seeping from the pelvic fractures, ruptured arteries are actively bleeding. At 11:32 a.m., I enter the interventional radiology operating room for an angio-embolization to stop the bleeding in the small hemorrhaging vessels.

Using a catheter under local anesthesia, Dr. James Park inserts a few artificial embolizing plugs made of gel-foam, along with a specialized coil, into the lower iliac and pudendal arteries. Through the catheterization, Dr. Park discovers my first "good" break: the shearing missed the larger, upper branch of the right iliac artery which, if severed, would have produced life-threatening blood loss.

Continuing in interventional radiology, urology performs a cystogram procedure of the bladder to locate and evaluate the extent of the bladder injury. It is critical to determine if urine is leaking out of my bladder into the pelvic area and creating the risk of infection.

With the pelvic bleeding under control and no threat of leaking urine, the trauma team continues its surgical plan for repairs to the diaphragm, pelvis, and bladder.

Meanwhile, on my end, there is no letup of the excruciating pain, even with intravenous pain medication. I am miserable and completely exhausted from distressed breathing and pain-wrenching transfers on and off gurneys and diagnostic tables. My doped-up mind struggles to decode medical acronyms and procedures I pick up from disjointed conversations on elevators and transports. However, my mind dials in clearly when I hear, "Prep her for diaphragm surgery."

Surgery, I know, will eliminate the pain, at least for the time being. At 1:05 p.m., I gratefully yield my body to the catatonic stupor that temporarily pulls the plug on my pain. Yes, anesthesia affords me a clean break from the present trauma, but it also blinds me to the living nightmare my loved ones begin to experience.

ALARMING SUPPORT

My sister, Nancy, a busy entrepreneur living in St. Petersburg, Florida, is taking a business call when my 10:45 a.m. call beeps in. I had just talked with Nancy the day before, so she lets my call go to voicemail. The 10:46 a.m. call to my neighbor Tricia is 7:46 a.m. in the state of Washington where she is on the road for the last hike of her outdoor vacation. Tricia's poor cell reception sends my call to voicemail as well.

Tricia retrieves her message first. Shocked and feeling helpless, she attempts to contact Nancy but can only leave a message for Nancy to call her. Nancy is alarmed with Tricia's vague message since Tricia rarely contacts Nancy. My sister intuitively thinks something must have happened and listens to my voicemail message reporting that I have been in a serious accident.

Within minutes, Nancy and Tricia connect and begin assembling a frantic long-distance support plan.

Imagining the worst, Nancy begins making calls to gather details about my condition. She is able to speak to the trauma unit at Mercy after an endless succession of phone menus, but only is told, "Paula is in surgery." Nancy then calls our brother, Jeff, who is at work and unable to talk. Frustrated, she contacts our cousin, Patty Steinle, desperate to find an available family member to advocate for me at the hospital. Lastly, Nancy contacts the Pittsburgh police for the accident report to determine the severity of the collision and if, or when, she should fly home to Pittsburgh.

As the startling information comes in, she realizes she must get home fast.

It was well after midnight, Wednesday morning, when Nancy landed, rented a car, and found her way to Mercy Hospital. In the meantime, Patty had unselfishly rearranged her Tuesday, arrived at the hospital in the early afternoon while I was in surgery and waited endlessly in the trauma ICU. Patty kept Nancy and Jeff informed with updates on the diaphragm surgery and let them know when I was in recovery. She then spent hours relaying the same information to other family members.

Best Laid Plans Don't Always Happen

While Patty waits and Nancy arranges her travel the afternoon of the accident, things get off to a good start with a successful diaphragm repair. Dr. Garth Elias, the attending general trauma surgeon, performs an exploratory laparotomy, a repair of the diaphragm injury, and an EGD (esophagogastroduodenoscopy).

The exploratory laparotomy is a surgical operation that opens the abdomen to examine the abdominal organs for injury or disease. The EGD is a scope procedure to examine the esophagus, stomach, and first part of the small intestine. Through the laparotomy and EGD, Dr. Elias learns I have no serious injuries to the upper GI and lower abdominal organs. What remains is the diaphragm repair. He discovers an 8 cm tear in the peritoneum nearest the heart and a bloodied diaphragm. He reinforces the tear with sutures and finally closes me up.

The trauma team is pleased that I tolerated the surgery well, which keeps me on schedule for more surgeries the next day. However, that evening my hemoglobin, hematocrit, and platelets drop critically low. Trauma ICU begins transfusing units of packed red blood cells and of platelets to prepare my body for the following day's surgeries. Ideally, the trauma team wants to complete the remaining surgeries as soon as possible.

Wednesday morning's surgical schedule has Dr. Gele Moloney, a trauma orthopedic surgeon, operating to reassemble my pelvis. In the afternoon, Dr. Ronald Benoit will repair my bladder.

At 9 a.m., everything remains on schedule and ICU sends me off to the OR prepped for surgery. Dr. Moloney is preparing to begin the pelvic repairs when suddenly my heart goes into unexpected atrial fibrillation with RVC's (rapid ventricular contractions), halting everything. Dr. Elias, the attending surgeon, delays the remaining surgeries and sends me back to trauma ICU until the cardiac complications resolve.

While in ICU, I remain intubated and placed on a mechanical ventilator in preparation for the remaining surgeries. The trauma team intentionally keeps me sedated to manage pain and prevent erratic movements that may cause further pelvic and bladder damage. Imagine my shock, during brief moments of consciousness, to awaken to the life-sustaining control of outside forces—arms tied down, a mechanical ventilator breathing for me, and a feeding tube up my nose. Luckily, I become conscious only a few brief times and each time find smiling faces of family and friends at my bedside providing words of encouragement.

Within 24 hours, my heart function improves enough to allow Drs. Moloney and Benoit to combine their separate procedures into one longer surgery the following day. By Thursday evening, my surgical repairs are finally complete. All that remains is to wean me from the ventilator.

A New Reality Sets In

Around midnight on Friday, September 16th, almost four days after the accident, I am free from the ventilator and on the other side of multiple critical surgeries. The fentanyl, which is10 times more powerful than morphine, is now replaced with less powerful opioids that keep me ahead of the pain and help me sleep. The thick fog from these drugs and the anesthesia are beginning to lift enough for me to get my bearings and survey the aftereffects of the accident. A glance at my body astounds me. I now understand the shock and anguish others feel when they first see what remains of their beloved home following a destructive tornado or hurricane.

Looking down my chest, I see dozens of staples extending 6" from the bottom of my sternum to my navel. More staples extend 6" from my navel to below my bikini line. Spanning hip-to-hip, I see a cumbersome ¾-inch metal bar and bilateral chunky connectors. These connectors stabilize ¼-inch titanium pins, which Dr. Moloney has drilled into each side of my pelvis. The pins extend outward 4" from my pelvis, the connecting bar about 3". The sight makes me queasy, and I feel like an alien creature. My mind fast-forwards to, *What type of clothes will I wear?* I don't yet realize that it will be months before I am out in public.

I later learn this bizarre device protruding from my body is called an anterior external fixator. Its purpose is to hold my realigned pelvis in place and inhibit me from twisting and bending forward. Right now, all that my mind can grasp is that I have a high-tech medical C-clamp squeezing me together while my glued pelvis dries.

Still surveying my body, I find bright bruises identifying all the pelvic fracture sites. On the right pelvis, stitches mark where Dr. Moloney strategically drilled a 4" screw to rejoin my separated sacroiliac joint. Looking to the left side, I find a 3" silicone drainage bulb wicking blood-like fluids from Dr. Benoit's bladder repair. I have a nasal cannula to increase my airflow and oxygen saturation levels. Both arms and wrists have dangling intravenous catheter ports; most are connected to running IV's.

The more I look, the more I find bumps, bruises, cuts, burns, and swelling everywhere. I am speechless as my mind tries to make sense of what is happening and the reasons for all these medical-support devices.

Just four days ago, I was an independent woman with a well-toned, athletic body. Now I don't recognize my body or know if I will be able to walk again. The drugs keep me from feeling pain, but I can still see that my body is broken, and I am bound to a hospital bed. It just does not add up in my mind. This isn't who I am, but it is what I have become.

I need time to piece together what occurred and understand what my future holds. No one is revealing much prognostic information; this concerns me. Family, friends, and my medical team all tell me I am doing well. Yet, to me being well is the farthest thing from what I am experiencing. I feel incredibly powerless to begin, or even consider, a journey back to health in this condition. I cannot imagine the strength and endurance it will take for me to recover all I have lost.

The overwhelming thoughts bring me to my limit. I am too exhausted to come up with a plan right now. All I can manage to do is close my eyes and sink into unconsciousness once more.

Maybe tomorrow things will be brighter.

3:01 a.m. Day 5; Trauma ICU—Bay 1

My glazed eyes are glued to the digital wall clock, watching as the seconds ever so slowly change. It takes what seems like minutes for 3:01:23 a.m. to become 3:01:24 a.m.

I am alone in the trauma ICU with no one to talk to except my drug-induced mind. For hours, we rehash the minutiae of everything I recall about the accident and the emergency interventions over the past four days. There is so much drama to work with that my mind and I create academy award-winning scenarios of what my unfortunate personal and professional future will be. Eventually, the endless thinking and widening depression wear me out. I fall asleep, still wondering which of the many questionable scenarios will claim the prize.

3.

STEERING FORWARD

THE HARDEST REALITY FOR ME TO ACCEPT is my body's state of brokenness. In 60 years of living, I never once experienced debilitating injuries like these. The worst I encountered was a broken finger, sprained ankle, broken jaw, and a few stitches, with each minor injury spread over decades of active living. This is the first time I am encountering this number of injuries, to this degree, all at once.

On one hand, this situation makes me realize how amazing the human body is. It is incredible that my body can take a beating like this and remain alive, plus muster up the energy to mend itself. I don't understand why I am alive, but I am so grateful that my body did everything in its power not to give up and yield to death. This unconscious and undying effort to continue living makes me wonder if my recovery has a more meaningful purpose aside from healing from my current physical state. I don't have any idea what that may be, but I do want to know.

CONTROLLING MIND GAMES

Don't get me wrong, there are certain things I can understand and handle in this situation. I won't be returning to work for at least a year—that just makes logical sense. I need time to heal and regain my strength. I can accept that I'll be unable to leave my house unassisted, given that there are steps at every exit. The part of this new reality I struggle hardest to accept is the idleness—being incapable of walking or doing any mundane household task while I wait months to become mobile again.

From my rehab background in orthotics and prosthetics, I know that for every day I am not moving, my body is susceptible to the health risks of immobility. This scares me.

According to the Registered Nurses Organization, the hazards of immobility affect seven organ systems: urinary, gastrointestinal, musculoskeletal, respiratory, circulatory, metabolic, and integumentary (skin). There is a domino effect with one decrease leading to another then to another since organ systems operate as a unit.

"What is going to happen to me?" I ask aloud for my body to hear. Instead, it is my mind that hears and responds.

You know your muscles will go first. This thought starts me picturing my musculoskeletal system shifting into reverse and backing down from the tip-top condition I had been actively maintaining. I try to estimate how many downward turns it will take, day by day, while I sit waiting for my fractures to heal. There is nothing I can do to change the wait, nor any shortcuts I can take.

Dark thoughts spiral. *What happens months from now when I do become mobile if I cannot be as active as before?* The possibility of chronic pain or nerve damage is unknown at this point. *What if my mind is right?* I think.

Before the accident, my identity was the "walk-her-talk" exercise physiologist and health coach with a lifestyle change coaching service. What if I can't do any of the physical things I enjoy most?

I love getting my hands dirty from gardening and home projects. I hike, bike, work out at the gym, and compete in women's basketball for the Senior Olympics. What if all this changes? Will I lose my credibility as a health coach? Will my intense enjoyment of life and these activities be gone?

My mind has me in its clutches now, and I can't stop questioning everything. *Do I have the gumption to believe I will regain my health and fitness again? How much atrophy will my body have one month from now? Two months? Will I be able to remain independent and take care of my demanding kitties and myself?*

These relentless dark thoughts spin me into a cavern of isolation. No one knows as intimately as I do the level of health and wellbeing I've lost. No one can understand the kind of joy and power I experience in being me, an independent, physically active woman. I need to get this back somehow.

Nausea sets in. It is not that others don't care. I have the most genuine and compassionate trauma team I can imagine. My family and friends are the best in the world. Yet, no matter how much compassion or medical expertise others extend to me, no one can make me "well" the way I want to be. They are incapable of knowing what my experience of wellbeing used to be, and they cannot make it magically happen for me. *I am all alone in this*, I think to myself.

WHAP! (Stars fly as these spiraling thoughts smack into a wall of awareness.) "Oh my gosh!" I say aloud. I just realized that since no one else can do it for me, the responsibility of creating my desired state of wellbeing is up to *me*.

As I think deeply about the responsibility being my own, a memory from the accident pops into my consciousness.

TAKING CONTROL OF THE WHEEL

I begin to recall in great detail the mystical Land of Oz experience in the car shortly after the collision. I remember the peace and joy I experienced and how detached my mind was from the pain and fear of the future. I remember the missing car doors, roof, and windshield and how everything around me seemed imaginary except for one thing. Clear as day, my hands were holding the tan-colored steering wheel of my Honda CRV at ten and two o'clock.

At the time, I did not question why I was holding the steering wheel or what that might mean. Now, suddenly it becomes clear, as though the bright light I saw in that magical place wants me to understand something important:

The primary purpose of a steering system is to allow the driver to guide the vehicle.

My jaw drops as this realization sinks in. The incidentals—car doors, roof, shattered windshield—were eliminated so I could see the powerful connection between a driver and the steering system. *I get it now! The steering wheel is meant to show me what I am to do.*

Thoughts stir again. *The steering wheel represents the way for me to regain the wellbeing I crave. It also means I need to get back into the driver's seat again.*

My mind redirects. *I am the only person who knows what I want to regain, and I'm the only one who can choose the direction my recovery takes. The steering wheel gives me the ability to stay on the road to recovery and travel as far as I am willing to go.*

Speed gathers. *I can be the planner, the designer, the owner of whatever I want my outcome to be in this new reality.*

Then, *WHOOSH!* I feel a shift of momentum. My thoughts are brighter and begin moving in a different direction that feels good—the opposite of how bad I was feeling.

New thoughts come at me from every angle. *Maybe the horrible reality I've been fearing isn't as bad as I think. I wonder if I can recover unlimited function if I figuratively take control of the steering wheel and choose to be the driver? Wow! I can dictate how "well" I want to become. I can deliberately steer myself in the right direction.*

"This is incredibly powerful!" I exclaim aloud.

DRIVING LESSONS

For the next few days, I shift away from doom-and-gloom thinking to the possibiities of being in the driver's seat of my new reality. The excitement of envisioning a positive future creates a noticeable positive energy about me. Friends and family comment on how good I look and how amazed they are that I am not depressed about the extent of my injuries.

I try to explain my steering wheel experience, but I can tell I am not conveying the essence of its power. I realize my ability to explain its meaning will improve as I understand it better myself.

So now, instead of watching TV when alone, I use the time to imagine what kind of control I gain when sitting in the driver's seat of my physical recovery. I start by analyzing the role of the vehicle, steering system, and driver since these were parts of my mystical experience. I wonder if there is a connection I need to understand about these interacting forces and the power they create.

I start with the vehicle because it reminds me of the body and how it operates. Each is a power-generating mechanism that relies on the driver to control how its energy is unleashed.

The steering system, on the other hand, is like the mind/body connection. It is an action-oriented conduit that moves the vehicle according to the driver's intentional turn of the steering wheel.

The more I think about these analogies, the more my appreciation grows for the power a driver has. The driver is the one in charge, the one who determines the vehicle's destination and the path to get there. *Isn't this similar to how my mind decides what I desire to have or be?*

This idea sparks another comparison: The driver makes quick decisions and reacts to potholes, traffic, and especially stops lights. This is similar to how I listen to my intuition to avoid getting hurt. I'm beginning to see I have many powerful options at my disposal if I choose to take on the driver's role in my recovery.

HIDDEN MEANING IN PICTURES

Nine days have passed and I am now out of the ICU in a private hospital room. My sister, Nancy, has been running around taking care of legal matters for me, including obtaining pictures of my car and the accident scene from witnesses. When I find out she has them, I insist on seeing them. Fearful that the pictures may upset me, Nancy tries to keep them from me but relents after my persistent hounding.

The photos of my car nearly bent in half jolt me. The repeated remarks from my medical team and others really begin to make sense now. "Most people, especially a 60-year old woman, would not have survived an impact like this," they tell me. Yet, somehow I did.

Seeing those photos makes me realize, without a doubt, that I survived the crash because of something more all-knowing than me. There had to be a Higher Power present that day that wanted me to have a second chance at living.

Too many "coincidences" happened to casually brush them aside: Darlene Anderson, a nurse living two doors away, is home and comes to my rescue; UPMC Mercy, a Level I Regional Resource Trauma Center, is located four short blocks away; my pelvis is sheered, but my iliac arteries are missed; and my sacrum is fractured, but my spinal cord and sciatic nerve are not permanently damaged.

These near-misses assure me I survived a horrific accident for a purpose. Is that purpose what I had been doing? Or is my life's purpose connected to this accident?

I cannot answer these questions with certainty right now. Instead, I tally up the metaphoric power the steering wheel provides me to deliberately "drive" the outcome of this recovery.

A few days pass while I think about who I am and the active life I desire to live again. These car-related metaphors make me realize I have more than enough power to rebound from all my injuries. But only if I rely on my body, mind, and spirit working together as the vehicle, steering mechanism, and driver to get me there.

Without hesitation I tell myself, *I'm choosing to get back in the driver's seat and drive this recovery.* The question now is, what specific outcomes do I intend to reach?

Principle 1
Embrace Your Power

While you must accept that your life and body now have a new reality, you still have the power to make choices and determine your own physical outcome. To rebound to the highest level possible, you must hold onto your power with all your determination. Although times of discouragement are inevitable, you always have the power to change.

Is the Glass Half-Empty or Half-Full?

This morning, I wake up with an unusual craving for coffee at breakfast. As soon as my food tray arrives, I grab the plastic mug, pry off the lid and raise it to my lips to take that anticipated first sip. It disappoints me when I look inside and find that the coffee fills the mug only halfway. Experience assures me it is pointless to press the call button and request more coffee since the rest of my breakfast will be ice-cold by the time it arrives.

I study what coffee I do have and realize I can look at satisfying my craving in one of two ways: I can see the mug as half-empty, feel cheated by what I did not get, and continue the day with a grudge. Or, I can see my mug as half-full and enjoy every wonderful sip of coffee the mug provides. With either choice I still get coffee.

4.

Is It My Mindset?

TODAY MARKS THE TENTH DAY since my accident and the fourth day since I began embracing the power I have to drive my recovery. I purposely keep mulling over my steering wheel experience to feel the tingle of energy it stimulates. Each time I mentally put myself in the driver's seat, I reassure my mind and body that I have the power to create a positive future.

Like one of Pavlov's dogs, I keep pressing the reward bar through my positive thinking because it makes me feel so good. Today though, I want more than to *feel* a sensation of hope. I want to *do* something that moves me forward in this bright, yet still invisible future.

It's yesterday's significant event that triggered me to strive toward something bigger. Physical therapy (PT) trained me to transfer my body across a slide-board onto a portable commode and into a wheelchair. To them, this is protocol. To me, it is a vista of normalcy appearing on the horizon sent from above.

Until yesterday, the closest "normal" activity I was able to do was sit up in bed or be transferred by Hoyer lift into a hospital recliner for a few hours. The use of a portable commode in place of a tiny bedpan feels epic, like Neil Armstrong taking that heroic "one small step."

Regardless of how momentous sitting on a portable commode feels, it is the experience in the wheelchair that is my "one giant leap for mankind" achievement. Occupying the seat of an actual wheeled vehicle transforms my figurative understanding of being the driver of my recovery into the experiential. Wheeling outside the confines of a hospital room and feeling the air hitting my face as my arms propel me resuscitates all my dormant senses. Movement has never felt so good!

The tingle I feel from tapping the embrace-my-power reward bar is nothing compared to the intensified surge the simple 36" x 10" slide-board produces. Mastering the slide-board allows me, *at will*, to get out of bed, sit in a wheelchair, and wheel around my room. I can pretend that I am engaging in the same habitual actions most people take for granted.

The addictive "I did it" feeling develops into an insatiable craving to embrace my power and apply it to even more deliberate action. I am stoked now to expand my capabilities and design what my new future will look like.

Déjà Vu Coffee Mug

When family and friends appear that afternoon, I proudly slide into my wheelchair and wheel myself around the bed to sit eye-to-eye and visit. Their reaction in seeing my wondrous feat multiplies my joy even more. Our conversations now shift away from, "How are you feeling today?" to chit-chatting about what is happening in their lives.

Most of my friends and family live active lives, so they catch me up on their recent hikes, dragon boat races, vacations, and gardens. As I listen, a déjà vu image begins bubbling its way to the surface of my awareness and I recall my initial reaction to the half-empty morning mug of coffee. When you are intensely craving something and are offered only a sliver of a taste, it quickly accentuates a half-empty perspective.

Tricia, my hiking buddy, tells me about the big oak tree that fell last night on Bradema Trail. Half listening, half thinking, I shake my head, "Oh yeah?" and mentally detach again to question my thoughts. *Yes, I remember being on that trail weeks ago. I wonder when I'll get back on Bradema. I really want to be hiking again, but who knows when that will happen. This really sucks!*

As more stories fly by, my thoughts return to the morning mug of coffee again, and I question myself further. So, how do I deal with being unable to do any of the activities my friends are doing? If I let these conversations sway me in a half-empty direction, I will begin resenting my injuries, my future, and even my friends. I don't like choosing which perspective to have; still, I don't want negative outcomes.

The high-energy surge I felt moments ago when showing off my sliding skills dramatically slows to a trickle as if my energy-hose is kinked. When I think about what I can't do presently, I feel deprived, especially when hearing about the fun my active friends are having.

The longer I stay kinked by feelings of envy, jealousy, and being cheated, the more I notice how less "good" I feel. All of a sudden, I am tired. My back is starting to ache and I'm having trouble paying attention. I tell my friends I need to rest, but actually, I just want to be left alone.

UNKINKING MY ENERGY FLOW

My friends graciously leave, and I am alone again with my nagging thoughts and battling perspectives. With both perspectives up for grabs, I decide to mentally review where I am in this healing process and what has just happened.

Let's see, I've been on this recovery journey for 10 days now. I have felt a rush of momentum each time I acknowledge my power to be the driver of my recovery. Yesterday, I had my first tangible experience of being a driver, albeit of a wheelchair. Today, I am sitting like a normal person talking with friends.

These positive thoughts unkink my energy, and I feel it flowing again, just not as strongly as before. I think I'm seeing a connection here between what I want and what I feel. I want more than anything to continue feeling better and better each day. And I know I feel the most energy when I focus on the new activities this slide-board allows me to do.

Suddenly, it's clear: All I have to do to keep my energy flowing is to envision the positive outcomes I want to regain in my recovery! Almost instantly, the Pavlovian habit-forming energy triggered by positive thinking gushes again.

After dinner two days later, my attending nurse tells me that the following day I am being discharged from UPMC Mercy Hospital to a UPMC skilled nursing facility called Seneca Place.

I've never visited Seneca Place but know it is in Penn Hills, about nine miles from Mercy Hospital by way of the Parkway East. I also know the drive there provides a picturesque view of the strenuous trails in Frick Park where Tricia and I like to hike. The route to the nursing facility also passes the exit I take to my home, which I haven't seen in over twelve days. All at once, I feel a kink of discontentment in my stomach and my energy diminishes…again.

From the palpable changes in my energy that repeatedly occur, I am recognizing a pattern between positive and negative thoughts and the feelings they create. I wonder what this means.

EXPANDING MY MINDSET

That evening, I pick up the *Psychology Today* magazine my friend, Sue, dropped off a few days earlier. My attention is caught by the article, "Mindsets," written by Gary Klein Ph.D., a renowned research psychologist on the subject of decision-making. The article is about thoughts, feelings, and the process we use to make important decisions that affect our lives or the lives of others. Dr. Klein explains that each of us develops personal viewpoints or temperaments from past experiences that predetermine how we respond to future situations. Klein refers to this mental and emotional framework as a *mindset.*

Reading further, I learn that Klein's research examines the way trained emergency professionals (trauma units, police, military) make high-stress decisions in life-threatening situations. Klein describes a mindset this way, "A mindset is a belief that orients the way we handle situations—the way we sort out what is going on and what we should do."

I find Klein's perspective of mindset thought-provoking. I had never thought of mindset as being closely tied to critical decision-making. I've associated mindset more closely with a general attitude or feeling a person has about something. For example, I have a positive attitude about fitness. I like the feeling of being fit and, therefore, I do fitness-oriented things. People recognize this in me and say I have a healthy mindset.

Klein's description of mindset, however, goes deeper than attitudes and feelings. He associates critical decision-making with strong beliefs formed from past experience that give us confidence we are taking the best action.

This causes me to reflect on how Mercy's trauma team had decided my emergency care. Team members were calm but intensely focused. Personally concerned, yet professional. They did not flinch at the number of injuries I had, and they figured out the best life-saving solution to every curveball thrown at them.

I make the connection with what Dr. Klein is saying: the trauma team confidently relied on their professional training and trauma experience to perform without hesitating.

But what about me? Will I be able to make the right decisions when it comes to getting well? What past experiences and beliefs can I draw upon to give me the confidence I am making the best decision in healing situations?

It's true I am the only expert who knows the level of wellbeing I want to achieve. And it is also true I have past experience in making myself healthy. It stands to reason I am the only one who can decide what my recovery will be. Using Klein's words, "how I sort out what is going on and what I should do" to manage my recovery will come from my *well-being mindset.*

This is an important realization. My wellbeing mindset is continually shaped by the beliefs I form from the good or bad emotions I experience. So when I chose to feel envy and jealousy the other day, my thoughts started to create a belief of being deprived of what I love most. This explains how my figurative mug began to appear half-empty. It also explains how those negative emotions zapped my energy and I began to feel pain and fatigue. The less I felt "good," the more negative thoughts I created and the worse I became.

"Wow!" I say aloud. "If I really want to reach my previous state of being well, I better pay attention to what I am thinking and *believing.*" I understand now how the dynamic works:

- My thoughts create vibrational energy that I feel as either negative or positive

- Either form of thought creates emotions—good or bad, happy or sad
- Repeated emotions become beliefs that influence actions
- Similar beliefs create a belief system or mindset
- My mindset directs my behavior and creates outcomes

Visualizing My Future

The very next day I begin expanding my wellbeing mindset to what I believe I can regain. In doing so, I begin to realize how different becoming well is from healing. I think many people see these two states as the same, especially when they believe doctors have the job of making them well.

I know from my background in exercise physiology and rehab that when our bodies are injured, they automatically begin to heal, regardless of whether we are paying attention or not. In other words, healing takes place without conscious effort.

Doctors create conditions for the healing to proceed optimally. For example, Dr. Moloney applied the external fixator to my pelvic bones so that they could heal in the proper alignment. Then, my body generated the energy that was knitting the bones back together. I did not have to do anything to make my bones heal.

Getting well is different. Achieving a personal state of wellness requires a patient to make a conscientious effort to reach a level of performance or quality of life that involves the body. In other words, the body follows the person's intention to be well, which increases its potential to heal beyond typical expectations.

I knew being treated in a Trauma 1 hospital meant that my body had been receiving the best care to enable it to heal. I also knew that my medical team would not be providing the type of care that would make me well. That part is up to me because it is driven by my wellbeing mindset.

Understanding the difference between healing and getting well makes me want more than ever for my body and my wellbeing mindset to work together. This is why I willingly do what I can to help my body heal while at the same time engaging my mind to make healthy decisions.

When I focus this way, I clearly see that when I deliberately imagine having the quality of life I want (instead of dwelling on what I don't have), I feel energized by the little things I can do. And I believe this is speeding up my body's healing.

As often as I can, I practice visualizing living life the way I want to live. I imagine as clearly as I can what it feels like to walk on Bradema Trail, shoot a free throw, or dig out my raised garden beds. The more I do this, the more all my senses come alive, and I swear I can smell the aroma of the crushed spearmint I just stepped on.

My coffee mug experience is a good reminder that I am the one deciding what I want or don't want by how I figuratively view how much coffee I find in my mug each day.

Tomorrow, I will begin the next leg of my recovery journey at UPMC Seneca Place. I am bound and determined to begin that day with a delightful *half-full* mug of coffee!

Principle 2
Envision Your Positive Outcome

Your thoughts and mindset determine outcomes. The more you can imagine the positive outcome of your rebounding effort with all your senses firing, the more likely you will manifest exactly what you imagine.

Mirror, mirror on the Wall, Who's the Most Independent One of All?

I just wheeled myself into the bathroom at Seneca Place to do my daily sponge bath. *Yep, one of these days I'm going to walk into my own bathroom and take a real shower!*

It has been almost a month since my auto accident, and when I peer into the handicapped tilt-mirror, the "mirror, mirror on the wall" lets me know it's time for a haircut. I mentally add another one-of-these-days to my growing list of abilities that I envision regaining in my mind each day.

While I'm conversing with the mirror, completely nude, the aide walks in and asks, "Do you need any help?"

I smile, desensitized to strangers talking to me while I am naked, and politely decline. I reply, "I have a system down pat now."

My system is to hold on tightly to *anything* I can do myself.

5.

A NEW KIND OF DANCE

"I'M GOING HOME!" I tearfully relay to my sister, Nancy, who is now back in Florida. The caseworker came in an hour ago to confirm that today is my last day in Seneca Place. Tomorrow, I will be transported by ambulance to my favorite place to be—home. It's been 31 days since I left for work the morning of September 13th. Part of me is out of my mind with excitement to step foot inside my beloved home, even if the stepping will be figurative.

The next morning, while double-checking my hanging closet and chest of drawers for potential left-behinds, I think about what it will be like to be home. I can't wait to run my bare feet across the plush living room rug and feel texture instead of cold institutional linoleum. I daydream about what it will be like to curl up on my living room couch, sleep in my upstairs bedroom, stand in my shower, and use a flushable toilet. I dearly miss BelGatto and Betsy Ann, my spoiled kitties, who I am certain by now have dismissed my services and are rubbing up against whoever's hand is feeding and caring for them. I am famished for the nourishing energy my home and kitties provide.

Still, I worry about how I will react to living in my home. Will I be happy and content, or will it upset me to be so close yet so far from living independently?

Living at home is going to be different. For the next few months, I will be limited to approximately 278 square feet of wheelchair access between three rooms. I'll continue using a hospital bed and a portable commode that will need to be dumped upstairs regularly since there is no bathroom on the first floor. Even though I will be able to wheel into my kitchen, I will not be able to cook. I might not even be able to open the refrigerator or get a drink of water at the sink.

My mental "mirror-mirror on the wall" tells me I will not be the most independent one of all, and I feel discouraged. *Review*, I command my mind. *Review what I want most!*

I answer myself aloud, "What I desire most of all is to attain the level of health and activity I had before." There, I said it. Somehow saying it aloud helps the mirror of my mind refocus, and I again see myself in the driver's seat regaining control. "I'm going home to heal!" I tell the mirror. "And life is going to get better."

A reassuring smile releases a surge of energy through me, similar to the one that came with my first wheelchair drive. Just then, there is a knock at my door and in walks the ambulance transport. "All set?" he asks.

"You better believe it!" I answer. "I'm going home!"

LOVED ONES TO THE RESCUE

Back in September, news of my auto accident went viral. Within a few days of the accident, Facebook posts, calls, visits, and an avalanche of cards, flowers, candy, and reading materials poured in and kept coming.

Family and friends from all over the world, some of whom I had not talked to in years, expressed their best wishes for a speedy recovery. These expressions of love had set off waves of healing vibrations throughout my body faster than any IV medication I received. If I could have bottled and sold this type of love, I'd be a millionaire.

I was surprised at how much people did for me. In the week before my final discharge, those closest to Pittsburgh banded together to address my living-at-home needs. My brother, Jeff, and hometown neighbors, Linda and Chester, cleared away furniture to make room for a hospital bed, portable commode, and wheelchair-width paths. Lisa and Schmaak put a meal delivery plan and sleepover schedule in place to buy time until *mia bella cugina* from Rome arrives to live with me.

Glenda Breth-Marcozzi, my first cousin on my dad's side, graciously accepted my request to live with me while I recover. Before the accident, Nancy and I had been planning to visit Glenda's family in Rome. Everyone agreed that in place of Nancy and me visiting the Marcozzi's, Glenda would visit here.

Glenda, however, cannot arrive until a week after my discharge from Seneca Place. To fill the seven-day gap, friends and family are pitching in to care for me. By the time the ambulance delivers me to my doorstep, everything I need will be in place. What a wonderful way to be welcomed home.

HOME SWEET HOME

As the transporter lowers me into my wheelchair, I am stunned by the transformation of my new living quarters. It has the look and feel of a hip New York City studio apartment, except that it's laid out for a disabled person. With deep gratitude, I tearfully say, "Thank you so much. I am finally in my home, sweet home!"

Within seconds inside the door, I can feel the positive vibes. Its familiar energy fills my parched soul like a shriveled sponge under running water. Tricia and Tina, who have just put the finishing touches on the recently-delivered medical equipment, shower me with welcome-home hugs. Susan is coming later to stay overnight; my refrigerator is stocked with meals and drinks; and all that remains is to practice maneuvering the new wheelchair in and out of my three rooms.

After briefing me on the meal and sleepover schedules and who will be stopping by to check on me, Tina and Tricia leave. Finally, I am alone in my home for a few hours before Susan's arrival. I slowly wheel around, taking in the sights and smells of my loving home and then park my wheelchair at the dining room table.

Looking out into my sunny backyard garden, I slowly inhale a deep full breath of my home's peaceful tranquility. Careful not to rush my exhale, I let my body absorb every iota of what I have missed while being away. I keep breathing and soaking up my home's restoring calmness while I reflect on all that I have been through since I left for work that September morning.

"I have come a long way," I say to my captive audience, BelGatto and Betsy Ann, who lovingly surround me. Returning home begins a new leg of my journey back to full health. This excites me. What does not excite me is still having to be dependent on others. Pausing to acknowledge that reality, I quiver, realizing there is no way around it. I must depend on others in order to continue getting well.

These thoughts make me catch my breath, making it strikingly shallow. My mind spirals with dismal thoughts of what my dependence means—no privacy, little solitude, and limited activities I can do on my own. My life at home will mostly consist of having people care for me while I do nothing but wait for my body to heal. My eyes begin darting back and forth in panic as I realize how horrible this could be.

Then, strangely, I happen to notice the glass of water Tricia left for me on the table. Of course, the contents measure about halfway. I laugh to myself as my thoughts slow down. It seems the Universe does not want me to lose sight of my power to choose what I want.

WHAT AM I RESISTING?

Swallowing a sip of water calms me a bit, but I feel a need to explore what is at the root of my twisted fears. "What is it about accepting help that causes me to feel smothered?" I ask BelGatto and Betsy Ann who look at me quizzically. "The people reaching out now are my friends, my family, people who love me unconditionally. They only want to help me get better. Why do I push back at having loved ones cook, clean, and take care of my needs while I recuperate?"

Betsy Ann jumps into my lap, and as I pet her, I think about how different my cats are from me. They *expect* to be taken care of and *accept*—at least for the most part—whatever I give them. As I continue to pet her, I realize I am used to being the one who cares for them as well as for my own needs. In fact, I am very capable of not only providing for my household but also for helping family, friends, and neighbors in need. What I realize I am *not* used to, is *being cared for.*

The fixator is the thing that complicates everything. Due to the location of the pelvic fractures, I cannot bear weight, bend forward, or twist too much for fear that the unstable fractures will displace. They are in a precarious stage now, where malformations can easily occur if I push beyond certain limits. It is in my best interest to be compliant, which means doing hardly any tasks I would normally do around the house. No doubt about it, I have to be helped by others; otherwise, I will hurt myself in the long run.

While listening to Betsy Ann purr, I consider what it may mean to be more like her—to expect and accept being helped. Lost in thought, five or more minutes go by as I continue stroking her, before I realize something important.

"So is it true that I don't want to accept other people's help?" I ask Betsy Ann.

No, that's not it. I fully understand the limitations my fractures present and acknowledge my need for help. Plus, I know those offering help are doing so out of the goodness of their hearts. It's got to be something about me. Maybe it's more about being the focal point of needing help. Whether I like it or not, this accident has made me the center of loving attention, which takes me out of my comfort zone.

"Yes, that's it." I blurt aloud, startling Betsy Ann.

I am uncomfortable receiving attention for the needs I can't meet for myself. I'm used to being the one helping others. In dead silence, I gaze around my dining room and think more about what I just realized.

Each of us seeks to be recognized for what we do—it validates who we are. I thrive on the type of attention I get from giving to others. However, in this scenario, I am the designated receiver. I have been chosen as the epicenter of a community of support that wants to express its love in helping me get well. I play a crucial role where the ultimate widespread effect of this outpouring rests on my acceptance.

My willingness to embrace this outpouring of help will open floodgates of love and healing so they flow freely in and out of *all* our lives. If I close the floodgates, for fear of feeling uncomfortable, I will shut myself and these giving hearts off from the experience of reciprocating love. Picturing the faces of the dear friends and family who are reaching out makes me consider the ramifications of these choices even more.

The deeper I reflect on my discomfort with accepting help, the clearer I understand that I've been focused on the wrong perspective. I've been preoccupied with *me*—my discomfort, my needs, my inabilities—*not* on what others are doing out of love for me.

If all I see is what I cannot do, I will feel harnessed, corralled, out of control of my life, and ultimately resenting help. If, instead, I envision myself recovering my self-care abilities and accept the temporary help that my support team is offering, I will feel free.

Indeed, these are two different patterns of thinking that produce polar opposite feelings toward receiving help. Right now, receiving help is the fastest way for me to reach the level of independent living I desire.

Staying focused on what I don't have is as satisfying as a half-empty glass of hot water on a sweltering day. All it does is make me unhappy and wanting more of what I don't have.

While I am lost in my thoughts, Betsy Ann jumps down from my lap and disappears upstairs, annoyed that I have stopped paying attention to her. I laugh, thinking, *Isn't that exactly what happens when we stop pay-*

ing attention to half-empty fears? They stop demanding our attention and disappear!

FINDING MY VOICE TO ASK

"Ding-dong, anyone home?" Susan announces as she pops in the door.

"Come on in and check out my new minimalist living quarters," I return, smiling. Susan is the first of six brave people who will stay overnight and care for me until Glenda arrives.

I mumble to myself as I wheel over to greet her, "How hard can it be to allow friends to help me now that I have cleared up my thinking?" Surprisingly, I find out just how difficult it is the very next morning when Susan comes downstairs.

"Good morning Susan, did you sleep well? We chit-chat for a bit while I muster up the courage to ask, "Um, when you get a chance…ah…would you mind doing me a huge favor?" I squeak out, my voice rusty and reluctant to ask for help. "Can you, um, can you please empty the filled bucket to my portable commode?"

I am surprised at how flushed my face becomes in asking.

Susan seems to think nothing of the request, but I feel embarrassed to the bone. While Susan scurries off with my bucket, I realize something sickening. I am going to recite this embarrassing request with everyone on the seven-day list, as well as with Glenda, until I am able to walk upstairs myself.

Sighing deeply, I think, *There has to be a more comfortable way of accepting help.*

LEARNING TO WALTZ

After seven days of awkwardly sponge bathing in plain sight and asking for my bucket to be emptied, I recognize this process of accepting help is like a sort of dance.

From ballroom and swing lessons, I remember that in order to flow, two individuals must work in unison, with one leading and the other following. My inability to be independent definitely positions me as the one who must follow, no matter how much I want or try to lead.

With my lame attempts so far, I resemble a bumbling beginner stepping on toes and awkwardly out of sync. Hopefully, my skills will improve with Glenda when she arrives on October 20th. For six weeks, Glenda will be my steady dance partner, helping me learn to become less stiff and more in step with asking for and accepting help.

Still, ever present in my mind is the day I can look into the mirror on the wall and know it is time for me to take the lead. For now, though, my humble role is to learn the tempo and flow of what it feels like to be led through the graceful waltz of receiving loving care.

The more I allow myself to be swept across the dance floor with ease, the more I will experience the transformative power available in working together with a caregiving partner.

In spite of how clumsy it feels right now, I truly want this to happen. I know my willingness to be a follower will enable me to regain my independence and no longer need to be led. But there is another benefit of perhaps even greater value. Whenever one of my loved ones needs a caregiving dance partner, I will know how to lead us in the most beautiful loving waltz of support.

Principle 3
Accept Help to Build Independence

Your healing depends upon accepting, rather than resisting the help of a supportive community while you work to regain independence as soon as possible.

HOW THE JOURNEY BEGAN

September 13, 2016: My car facing opposite the intersection after ricocheting off the second rowhouse.

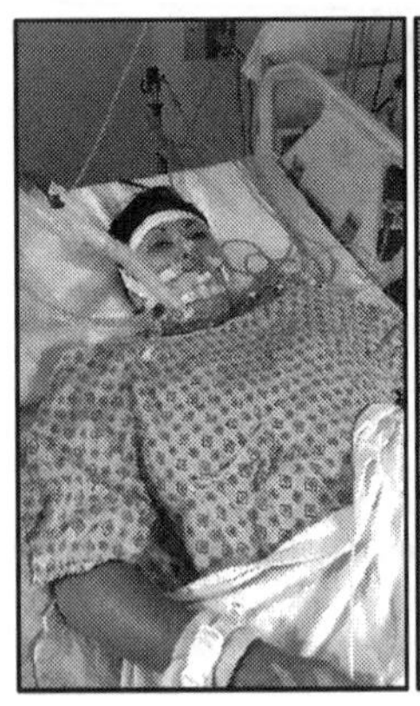

UPMC Mercy Trauma & Burn ICU.

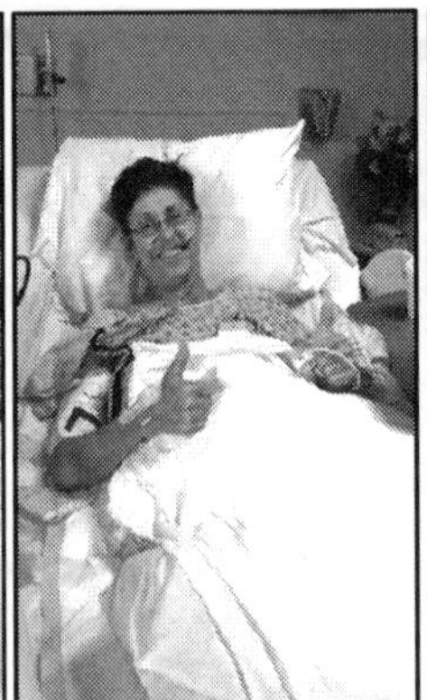

Mercy Stepdown.

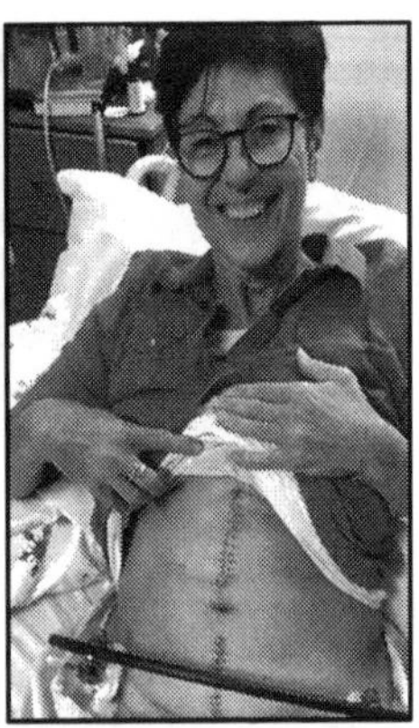

Seneca Place skilled nursing and fixator.

REHABILITATION

Dr. Gele B. Moloney, pelvic trauma surgeon, and me.

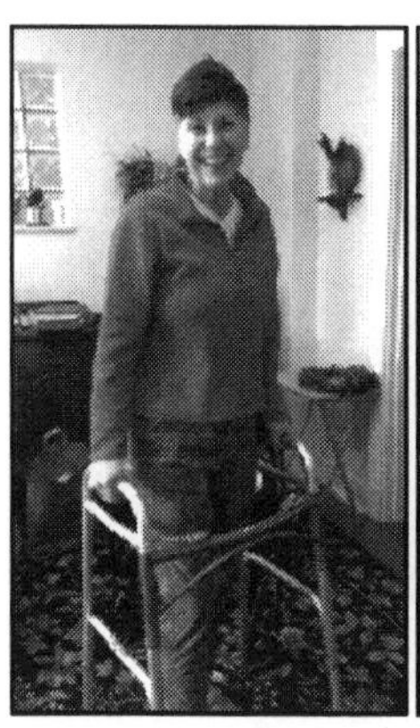

November 2016 post fixator removal.

Out in my garden.

December 2016 Frick Park.

Mistaken Identity

"I'll pull up to the curb," my friend, Joanie, says.

"And I'll bring your wheelchair and slide-board around to your door," Glenda pipes in.

Minutes later, I'm wheeling myself through the door of the Monroeville Target, animated as a kid entering the Magic Kingdom in Disney World. This is my first excursion in public, besides trips to Mercy Hospital for progress exams with Dr. Moloney. However, no matter where I look, I notice the stares from people of all ages.

What are they looking at? I wonder. Is it the XX-large men's sweatpants pulled over my protruding external fixator? Is it my hair showing blatant gray roots? Or is it that I am the disabled woman in a wheelchair?

Possibly, they are looking at all three. Nevertheless, I don't let the stares stop me. I am soaking up every second I have outside the four walls of my tiny home.

6.

BRIDGING THE GAP

THE THRILL OF BEING HOME, sliding in and out of bed, on and off a portable commode, and into my wheelchair has gone flat. What once had me riding a wave of achievement has become ho-hum ordinary. I am bored out of my mind with the three abilities I can do and weary of my home—the one place I could not wait to have back. I crave to see more than four walls, more than what I view outside my windows or sitting on my deck. I need something to confirm that I am becoming well—more than knowing my body is healing.

The easier it becomes to perform the limited skills I have mastered, the harder it is to graciously accept help from anyone. Poor Glenda, sometimes I unconsciously blurt out abrupt words when I am frustrated with myself and my situation. The petty things I notice have nothing to do with her. I am venting the pent-up annoyance of being confined to this wheelchair and unable to do the things I enjoy.

I want to be the one who whips up antipasti for friends who drop by unexpectedly in the middle of the afternoon. I want to cook dinner for family and friends who have helped me while in the hospital. I feel demanding when I ask Glenda to do what I would do if I were not in a wheelchair. I hate that all I can do is sit and watch others run my household. I wish I had someone to talk to who understands exactly what it feels like to be confined to a wheelchair.

Things will improve on November 9th, I think to myself, somewhat convincingly. On that day, less than 48 hours away, Dr. Moloney will surgically remove the external fixator. Going to the hospital will not only be a change of scenery; I will also come home freed from the limitations of that annoying fixator.

With the fixator removed, I'll be able to bend forward, sleep curled up on my side, and best of all, stand. It has been 57 days since I stood. Seeing life from above wheelchair height will be an ecstatic experience. I can't wait to look people square in the eye, hug standing up, and see the bottom of my kitchen sink. Surgery day cannot come soon enough!

A New Independence Day

As soon as I have my wits about me in recovery, the first thing I do is feel for the fixator. Gone! No more clunky bar to bang into. I roll onto my side and ease my way into a satisfying fetal position. Perfect! Although I just woke up, I can't wait to go to sleep tonight. This may be my first night of restful sound sleep since the accident. No more having to sleep on my back and no more stiff neck.

In the consulting room, Dr. Moloney tells Glenda that the surgery went well. The doctor believes my pelvis is stable enough to support a limited amount of vertical weight bearing. As a result, upon discharge from recovery, the orderly transports me in my wheelchair to the physical therapy department to be fitted with a walker. Glenda and Joanie, who drove us, tag along, and we chat up a storm about which new activity I will do first without the fixator.

When my turn comes, the physical therapist (PT) approaches with a walker and starts right into demonstrating the technique of ambulating with a walker.

"What?" I say to her, bewildered. "You mean that I am not here just to receive a walker, I'm actually going to use it?"

"Absolutely," the PT says, smiling reassuringly. She goes on to explain that I am to bear 100 percent of my weight on my left leg and to only lightly touch down on my right side on each step.

I barely hear what the PT is saying. Instead, inside me waves of emotion swirl between sheer excitement and deer-in-the-headlights fear. *I can't believe I am about to walk. What will it feel like to stand up? I wonder if it will hurt to have weight on my pelvis or my legs.*

I'm not sure my arms are strong enough to hold me while I swing forward.

Everything around me is moving at warp speed. The PT is adjusting the legs of the walker while reviewing the technique. Glenda is queueing up her phone camera to record this memorable feat. Joanie is rounding up a crowd of supporters, and I am lost in fear.

"1-2-3 and up," we say in unison as I push off the wheelchair arms and lean forward onto the walker. "Wow! That was not as hard as I expected." The walker teeters a bit as I sway forward and backward, trying to find my balance.

"So far so good," I say, smiling.

Before attempting my first step, I gaze around in wonderment, unable to believe how tall I feel. I think, *Gee, now I get how Peg (my 6-foot basketball teammate) sees things.* Looking down, everything, especially my feet, seems so far below me. I marvel at what a room looks like from a standing perspective.

The PT urges me to take a few steps forward, mindful to not put more than 2-5 percent of my weight onto my right foot. It's been so long since I had any weight on either foot that I have no idea how much 2-5 percent is. I figure it's better to err on the safe side so I let my arms bear the full weight of my body as I swing forward.

Before I know it, I have traveled 20 feet across the room. I am exhausted and thrilled at the same time as I plop back into the wheelchair. "That was great," the PT says and tells me our lesson is over for the day.

"Is this a dream or did I actually walk 20 feet?" I ask. Glenda assures me that indeed I did. She shows me the recorded "first walk," which to me looks nothing like walking and more like a monkey swinging on a walker.

Grinning from ear to ear, I tell the crowd Joanie gathered, "This day will go down in history as one of my most cherished memories. This morning I was freed from the fixator; I walked 20 feet; and tonight I will sleep like a baby! Life is good!"

MY BOSOM BUDDY WALKER

One day, to humor myself, I do an inventory of the collection of assistive devices I have. Added to a hospital bed, portable commode, slide-board, reach grabber, sock aid, leg lifter, incentive spirometer, and wheelchair, I now include a walker. It's a fancy walker with wheels on the front and nice grips. It also folds up easily.

Dr. Moloney's orders permit me to use the walker to whatever level I can tolerate as long as I put little weight on my right leg. *This is wonderful,* I think, *just the incentive I need to feel like I am progressing toward becoming well.*

My new bosom buddy, the walker, gives me choices I didn't have before. I laugh to myself, thinking about how this inanimate aluminum contraption has power to awaken a sense of autonomy in me. I can now exercise my right to sit, stand, or walk a few steps whenever I want.

The next day, my home PT, Maryann, asks me to "walk" into the kitchen, out through the dining room, and into the living room—we estimate this is a distance of about 20 feet.

My "I did it" thrill comes bursting through just as it did in the hospital PT department. More proof that I am regaining the life I want.

Each victorious walk, however, reveals how deconditioned my body is. I cannot tolerate more than a few minutes of being vertical before my arms and left leg tire or begin to ache. Still, I am content to do many sets of shorter walks because I know, from being a personal trainer, that multiple baby steps produce the best results.

My strategy is to string together short stints of standing or walking throughout the day. I can tell my body has forgotten many of its natural responses. Somehow, my body and mind need to reawaken to the feeling that standing and walking are a thoughtless action rather than a planned event. To do this, my endurance, strength, and balance need to improve so I can make better use of the support my assistive tools provide.

"And Paula," Maryann says, "In another week you should graduate to crutches and learn how to go up and down stairs."

My eyes sparkle with delight since this means I can break loose from being homebound and go places! Dr. Moloney has predicted that by the first of the New Year I can put full weight on my right leg. By mid-January, I should be using only a cane.

Each time I envision my activity-building future, my eyes well up with tears. I am becoming *well*, and no longer just healing! All the days I spent saying to myself, *What I desire most of all is to attain the level of health and activity I had before,* have paid off. It is actually happening now.

YOU DON'T KNOW UNTIL YOU TRY

I never imagined how much I could appreciate an assistive device, such as a walker, to make me feel more independent. I recall how many patients resisted using tools like these during my early career as a prosthetist and orthotist. They cited a variety of reasons, but the two most common were 1) not wanting to be seen as being handicapped; and 2) not feeling confident using the device. Now that I have firsthand experience being dependent on assistive devices, I understand how easy it is to develop a resistance toward using them.

The social sting of being perceived as disabled burns. On the rare occasions when I was in public with my wheelchair, I could not help but notice the inquisitive stares.

People non-verbally expressed genuine kindness toward me by opening doors and allowing me to go ahead of them. I could sense they wanted to know my situation, and some even struck up a quick conversation, but they never asked about the wheelchair. Our interactions were polite. Strangers would cordially smile as they looked down at me, and I would graciously smile back up at them. It may have been only my perception, but the interaction made me feel *less-than.*

In my mind, I am not disabled, although technically, I suppose I am. I see myself on the road to a full recovery, so why don't others? I presume the only evidence bystanders have to formulate an opinion is by what they see—my appearance of disability.

As I reflected on these experiences one evening, I made a vow to myself to always see others with disabilities for who they really are and not by what their affliction appears to be. I also decided I would focus on who I really am. I told myself, *I won't allow people's misperceptions to dissuade me from my wellbeing plans. I am going to fill my mind with thoughts of walking normally, running, jumping, and hiking, rather than thoughts of what others might presume to be my situation.*

Still, I can't argue with the physical reasons patients do not feel confident using assistive devices. These supports are downright clunky, unnatural, and tipsy. It takes a great deal of practice and effort to feel any sense of control.

The real or perceived sense of falling makes it easy to cut any corner of technique recommended to maintain stability. The only problem is, cutting corners can form bad habits of gait. Because I don't want to develop bad habits of walking, getting good at using whatever device I need is a must.

Lying in bed one night, I think about how fortunate I am to have a background in the biomechanics of walking as well as knowledge of anatomy and physiology. I understand what Maryann means when she tells me where to shift my weight to gain more stability. I know to pay attention to my posture so I don't add more muscular imbalances to the ones I already have. I have no idea what other patients do who don't understand how to leverage their body movements to their advantage.

Still, in spite of what I know, I too have to build confidence in the support these devices provide. The fear of pain or falling is real and very distracting. Each time I practice, a tug-of-war goes on in my mind between the possibility of falling and the need to build my skills and strength. Part of me does not want to gamble on falling while the other part keeps cheering me on to regain more function. It's a nagging choice I have to make again and again.

Maryann says that she can tell right away those patients who will walk normally from those who won't by how they overcome the fear of using their supportive device. I don't want fear to stop me. I would hate it if the fear of falling kept me from a breakthrough in higher function, especially if I was inches away from gaining an advantage. I tell myself, *I'm going to practice using my waker until I am perfect at walking again.*

As soon as I make this commitment, my mind goes back to a class I took as an undergraduate at Penn State. One of my health and physical education professors, Dr. Ralph Sabock, challenged the collective belief in the well-known adage, practice makes perfect.

Dr. Sabock asked, "Is it true? Does practicing something make you perfect at it?"

Being naïve students, we unanimously responded, "Of course it does."

I have never forgotten his reply. Dr. Sabock said, "Practice only makes permanent. And if you practice something imperfectly, it will become permanent, not perfect."

Dr. Sabock, of course, is right. I can choose to mindlessly practice doing what Maryann tells me, or I can perfect my ability to walk each time I practice.

I decide that I'm going to practice perfectly because I want more than anything to be as active as I can be—both perfectly and permanently!

Principle 4
Leverage Assistive Devices

Relying on assistive devices is a path to independence rather than an admission of disability. Don't hinder your recovery by resisting this type of support.

Harvesting a Bum Knee

"Congratulations Paula, you've graduated to crutches!" Maryann, my PT, says. "Remember, as you use your crutches, put all your weight on your left leg and hardly any on your right leg."

"Will do, Maryann," I say cheerfully.

As soon as she leaves my house, I immediately crutch my way down the deck steps and out into my backyard garden. Both Glenda and I shed tears as I say, "I can't believe I'm standing in my garden!"

Thanksgiving is a week away, and because of an unseasonably mild fall, I still have cold weather plants thriving. After thoroughly inspecting everything and deciding what is ready to harvest, I limp up the four steps to my deck and collapse in my wheelchair.

Looking down, I discover my left knee has doubled in size. Shrugging it off, I try to convince myself, *Oh, I guess a few hours on crutches are too many. It will be better tomorrow*. The next morning, however, my knee is still doubled in size. Days later, it is still swollen. Disappointed, I resign myself to making an appointment with my orthopedic surgeon, Dr. Moloney.

7.
POSITIONED TO WIN

"YOUR LEFT KNEE X-RAYS show no fractures, but there is joint effusion (fluid on the knee). Let's get an MRI to find out why," Dr. Moloney says in the exam room.

As soon as the MRI report posts in my portal, I open it with trepidation. My eyes quickly scan the lengthy report and fix on the "impressions" section at the bottom. As I read it in detail, my half-full glass of high hope for continued progress goes bone-dry empty.

"Oh no!" I exclaim. The MRI impression states a partial medial collateral ligament (MCL) tear; bone bruises to the medial femoral and tibial condyles; micro-fractures of the fibular head; and a posterior lateral meniscal tear.

It appears the automobile accident has struck again. The impact's lateral force damaged my left knee by bending it in an abnormal L-shaped angle that put intense strain on the medial side of my knee. Because I hadn't been bearing weight on my knee, these injuries had gone unnoticed.

I swallow hard in disbelief. All my plans for a gradual build-up of vertical weight bearing are set back indefinitely. My chest droops as tears roll down my cheeks. I've only been vertical less than ten days since the fixator was removed, and now this.

This setback sinks my spirits to the lowest point since the accident. Slumping in my wheelchair, I stare at the screen, trying to accept that I must use the wheelchair *more* rather than less while my knee heals. Using the walker and crutches the way I planned will only aggravate these injuries.

Dr. Moloney's treatment recommendation is conservative, advising me that these types of knee injuries usually heal on their own. But my patience for taking a wait-and-see approach has run dry. To my activity-hungry mind, the knee injuries are worse than my pelvic fractures. I need to be 100 percent dependent on this injured knee to go up and down stairs until I can begin using my right leg in January.

I grumble to anyone who will listen, "I don't want to add more healing time to my already lengthy recovery. Besides, why haven't these injuries healed already? I spent 57 days with no weight bearing."

In one last-ditch effort to find a more favorable solution, I call two of my physical therapy friends, Nancy Foley and Lori Wynn. Maybe Nancy or Lori can work some magic and provide tips to heal these injuries faster. Unfortunately, they both agree with Dr. Moloney and assure me that with time, ice, and limited use, these knee injuries will heal without surgery and that I can resume pursuing my long-range recovery goals.

They also explain that the knee injuries didn't heal fully while I was in the wheelchair because I was sitting rather than bearing weight. The action of flexing and extending a knee while bearing weight pumps synovial fluids rich in healing properties through out the knee. My PT friends encourage me to keep using the walker and crutches but to be conservative.

REBOUNDING

It takes a few days for me to finally accept these injuries as my new reality. *Come on, Paula, you've been down this road before*, I remind myself as I recall what I learned from my steering wheel experience. I decide to humbly climb back into the driver seat and apply this conservative solution to my disappointing setback.

Gee, this is my first major setback and I've already crumbled. What will I do with the next one? I'm sure there will be more since I don't have just one injury that is healing. My entire body needs to heal and then relearn to work again as a unit. I tell myself, *Paula, you have a very long obstacle-ridden road ahead of you, so you better figure out a way to rebound from setbacks.*

I'm not sure what made me say the word *rebound,* but whatever it was, the word registered immediately. Rebounding can be interpreted in a few ways, but I tend to think of it in terms of rebounding in basketball, a sport near and dear to my heart.

Being one of the shorter players on our 60's+ Senior Olympics women's team, I love it when I am able to get a rebound off a much taller opponent. As our basketball coach, Bill Lahr, explains, "It's all about how you position yourself."

Bill preaches that positioning your body between the basket and your opponent gives you an inside advantage for getting the ball after a missed shot. When you get the ball, you get another chance to score, and scoring points determines a positive outcome.

Okay, I know how to effectively rebound in basketball. Now I just need to understand how to position myself advantageously when a setback occurs.

I recall learning from a behavioral change specialist course that our experiences—good or bad—result from our unique patterns of thinking, feeling, and behaving. Maybe paying attention to my thoughts and feelings could be a way to position myself to rebound from setbacks.

I decide to experiment with what happens to me when I pay close attention to the emotions I have during the day. What do I feel when I see myself making progress as well as when I hit small hurdles?

I record my feelings over five days and discover that I experience a distinct joy when I see any type of improvement. I also find there is an unmistakable feeling of discouragement when I go backward, even slightly. In fact, my left knee hurts more when I think I'm regressing.

This gets me thinking. If I apply Dr. Sabock's wisdom to perfectly practice imagining myself walking, running, and playing basketball, I can generate good feelings which will keep me focused on seeing progress. I wonder what repeated bouts of feeling good each day will do for getting me through this setback?

I decide to find out. I'm going to track my thoughts, feelings, and behaviors to see what outcomes I get over the next month.

FINDING MY BEST POSITION

At this point, Christmas is a week away. Glenda has returned to her family in Italy, and my sister, Nancy, is caring for me until after the New Year when I will be fully weight bearing. I've progressed to climbing stairs, sleeping in my own bed, and even taking a one-legged standing shower. I split time between using crutches, the walker, and the wheelchair to be mobile, and I use the portable commode to avoid climbing stairs more than once a day.

Nancy and I joke that although I am capable of leaving the house on crutches, I am eternally slow and drag along accessories that make any trip with me a journey. Therefore, for quick runs to the store, Nancy is much happier to go alone, even though she doesn't have me to navigate unfamiliar roads. Nancy's solution is to rely on iPhone's Siri that uses GPS (Global Positioning System) for directions.

I am fascinated by how navigational GPS works. The GPS tracking unit and multiple satellites somehow communicate with one another to instantly calculate precise proximity to a preprogrammed destination. Today's GPS tracking units are integral parts of cell phones, smart watches, and computer systems. Whether or not we choose to use or even acknowledge it, global positioning is constantly working and available.

What intrigues me the most is the personal choice we make to be guided by some lightning-speed transmitting system. Before the accident, I used satellite navigation regularly while driving to unknown destinations. Trusting that GPS could see the best route more clearly than I did, I was confident I would arrive at my destination.

My preoccupation with figuring out a way to rebound from setbacks has me wondering if it is possible to rely on a type of *internal* GPS to navigate my recovery.

I see many similarities between navigational GPS and the guiding insights I have adopted so far in my recovery. For example, there is a driver—and that's me. I have envisioned a positive outcome, which is my preprogrammed destination. I have the means of getting there by accepting help from my community of support and assistive devices. And most recently, I learned there will be unexpected detours or setbacks that I will need help navigating around.

So, all I need to figure out is how the rest of an internal guidance system would operate.

To start, there would need to be an outgoing signal to identify where I am. *Okay,* I say to myself, *how do I typically signal what I am thinking and feeling? By words!* My spoken words express what I am thinking and feeling and act as signals that "position" my stance on whatever is of interest to me.

But what if I don't express my thoughts in words? What if I hold them within? I realize that I still send signals with my expressions, emotions, and actions. *So,* I conclude, *I guess I am always sending out signals through what I think, say, and do.*

I review the emotions I have monitored over the past few weeks and see a strong connection between what I am feeling and what I do. I notice that when I have a good day, I feel confident I am doing the right things and moving closer toward my goals. On those days, I often tell others, "I feel better," and I notice I am more productive.

When I have a not-so-good day, I usually tell others, "I don't feel that great." I become discouraged and quickly think something is not right or that I'm doing something wrong. I feel defeated, my pain increases, I feel tired, I take more pain medication, or I stop doing exercises for a few days. Figuratively speaking, I get detoured or lost, which only adds more time and distance to my recovery destination.

This makes perfect sense. My thoughts are the signals going out, and my emotions are the messages coming back, revealing the direction I am taking. This is something I am already paying attention to, and I know it is trustworthy.

But, what about me represents the all-seeing satellite that constantly knows where I am and the best path to take?

What inside me is ever-present, intelligent, able to see beyond what I can see, reliable, concerned for my safety, and patiently recalculating the best way to my desires?

I spend a few days exploring this question and wondering if this guidance system is my mind. Or, is it my body-mind connection? No, this type of guidance feels much larger, broader, and unlimited than just those two aspects of myself. What else could it be? By thinking beyond the obvious, it dawns on me that this internal guidance system is the complete mind/body/spirit connection that is within us all.

Everything I have ever read about wellbeing supports that we are much more than our physicality. Our total being also includes our thoughts, emotions, and our spirituality. These combined elements give us an identity, determine our health, and make us who we are.

"Of course, that's it!" I shout aloud. My mind/body/spirit connection knows intimately everything I desire to regain and will definitely lead me in that direction. That is *if* I choose to listen to it. I know how easy it is to be distracted and ignore my GPS's instructions in the car.

I want more than anything to get well, and I am willing to pay attention to my thoughts and emotions and listen to my mind/body/spirit internal guidance system. Not only can this part of myself direct me to my recovery destination, but more importantly, I know it will tirelessly redirect me when I get detoured with setbacks.

Realizing I have this support system couldn't come any sooner. When Nancy leaves on January 4th, I will be totally on my own for the first time since the accident. The best way for me to keep progressing, regardless of whatever setback appears, is to have a dependable and trustworthy internal system to guide me.

To make my mind/body/spirit internal guidance system even more tangible to me, I decide to give it a name. I call it my *Rebound Positioning System*, or RPS.

Similar to a GPS, the RPS uses my thoughts and emotions to let me know if I am on the right road, leading to the envisioned health outcomes (destinations) I desire. I can tell I am heading in the right direction when what I am doing feels good. The opposite is true as well. When what I am doing makes me feel bad or unhealthy, I know I am heading off track.

If I listen to my RPS, I will not only keep moving forward, but I will also be in the best position to respond quickly to any setback.

No matter if our basketball team is winning by twenty points, we can always hear Bill, our coach, screaming from the sidelines, "Box out on every shot." I never realized how dead-on accurate he is. Consciously positioning yourself to gain control is all about setting yourself up to win.

Bill, you're a genius!

Principle 5
Expect and Rebound from Setbacks

Setbacks are an inevitable and natural part of recovery. Facing each setback with humility, self-reliance, and acceptance enables you to keep moving forward at a realistic pace.

Standing at the Crossroads

"I'm going to miss you," I sob, hugging Nancy as she leaves for the airport the morning of January 4, 2017. Watching Nancy walk away, a queasy wave rolls in my stomach as I realize the most fearsome leg of this recovery—living alone—is about to begin.

I've intensely dreamed this mile marker would come, and now that it is here, shadows of apprehension are eclipsing my courage. Am I ready to face the scary unknowns this phase of recovery brings? Moving forward is risky. Standing still seems safer, but it comes with the cost of sacrificing my goal. *Which will it be, Paula? Play it safe or risk more to gain more?*

8.

Green Light Means Go

"HELLOOO?"

A hollow echo of my voice responds. I never knew my house to sound cavernous like this. I suppose I got so used to the bustling noises of people coming and going that, now that I am alone, it sounds eerily quiet.

"What's on your agenda today, BelGatto?" I ask my black kitty, who is kneading his plush bedding, preparing it for his *next* nap. "Never mind, I already know."

What's on *my* agenda is the better question. Before she left, Nancy did laundry and stocked me with staples to last at least a few weeks. Everything is in place, leaving me the rest of the day to do…well, what will I do?

Besides daily exercises and feeding myself and the cats, there is nothing pressing for me to do. My life exists in an uneventful limbo, waiting for healing to finish. Maybe when I see Dr. Moloney in a few weeks my world will expand. I am hoping she will release me to drive.

GETTING THE GREEN LIGHT

At my appointment with Dr. Moloney nearly two weeks later, she says, "Your pelvic X-rays are looking good. The fracture sites are callusing and have not displaced. These are all good signs that things are progressing as planned."

I grin and quickly ask, "So what about driving? When can I start?"

Dr. Moloney thinks, then gives me a thumbs up, but follows with a word of caution. "Take it slowly. Physically you should be fine; however, you may find some psychological issues surface."

"Okay," I say, half listening.

I leave Dr. Moloney's office with a prescription for outpatient physical therapy and an insatiable itch to drive. All the way home on the bus, I think about taking a very *short* first drive to Trader Joe's for some much-needed groceries.

On blind faith, I had bought a new car just before Christmas so Nancy and I had a mode of transportation. I jokingly told Nancy, "I hope that when the time comes for me to drive, I like this car as much as you do."

"I guess I find out now," I chuckle to myself while climbing into the driver's seat. With my cane nestled in the passenger seat, I start the engine for my first solo drive in over four months.

Trader Joe's is just 2.5 miles from my home. In the hundreds of times I have driven there, I have never before noticed that there are eleven traffic lights each way. Before the accident, traffic lights were annoying hindrances that lengthed any drive. Now, these same lights seem like living, ghoulish beings that are preying on me.

It is inevitable that I am stopped by some of the eleven red lights. Worse still, is when I'm the first car through the intersection when the light turns green. No matter how hard I try to stay focused, my mind flashes back to the corner of Jumonville and Forbes the morning of September 13, 2016. With each new green light, my body constricts automatically, bracing itself to be rammed by a distracted driver running his or her red light.

My hypervigilance intensifies with each red light intersection, turning me into a threat to other drivers. Horns blow as irate drivers speed by, making me feel more paranoid and disorientated while I try neither to be the cause nor the victim of another accident.

By the time I reach home, I am a mental and physical wreck. I leave my groceries on the kitchen floor and collapse on the couch for a few hours to settle my shaking body.

What just happened to me? I wonder, dumbfounded.

A DEFINING MOMENT

I never anticipated my first drive to be this debilitating. Sure, I thought I'd be a little nervous, especially driving a new car with an unfamiliar dashboard. But my experience went beyond being nervous—I panicked. Racing heart, shortness of breath, sweating, blurred vision—I had all the classic symptoms of a panic attack, something I'd never experienced before.

The baffling part is, I don't understand why driving took control of my body this way. This driving experience supersedes any of the frightening emotions I remember encountering in my recovery before today. In ICU, there were the frightening, spiraling thoughts as I learned the extent of my injuries and what they might mean for my future. Then there was the anxiety of living with people at home and the embarrassment of asking for help. I remember how scared I was to take my first walk and the hesitation when I first went down the stairs on crutches, anticipating a tumble.

All of these experiences caused me fear, but they didn't control me in the same way as taking a short drive did.

I search my past to find a pattern that could explain my new panic and its impairment on my driving skills. I begin to see a connection forming between self-confidence and my ability to learn a new skill or adjust to a new situation. I am a quick study when it comes to learning practically any new skill. As my confidence about my ability to perform a skill-based task grows, fear of failure has less of a hold on me.

That is why I hadn't been controlled by fear up until now. My depth of knowledge, abilities, and determination to use my body to ambulate all work together to make me self-confident. Now, I see how driving is different.

Driving in traffic is not based only on *my* confidence or skills. It includes other people's skills, knowledge, and determination to drive however willfully they choose. No matter how skillful I am or careful to obey traffic laws and speed limits, I cannot guarantee another driver will do the same.

The panic surrounding driving now makes perfect sense: other drivers take me out of my element of self-reliance and make me feel powerless.

I realize that overcoming this fear is going to require more than having confidence in my abilities since it also involves interacting with other drivers. I must somehow learn to face the emotional fear of getting hurt by other drivers.

I wonder, how do I do this?

Almost as if my Rebound Positioning System (RPS) was queued to respond, something I once heard pops into my mind and redirects my thinking:

We are not defined by what happens to us.

We're defined by how we respond to what happens to us.

My eyes well up with tears as I think about how this relates to me.

I do not want this accident or fear of being harmed by other drivers to define me as powerless and vulnerable. Instead, I want to expose and face head-on all the real or imagined fears that immobilize me. I want my recovery to be defined by how I have learned to overcome my fears.

Tears drip onto my chest while a wave of joyful goodness ripples through me to confirm I am on the right track. "Okay," I blurt aloud, "now that I know the direction I want to take, how do I do this?"

ATTRACTING HELP

Early the next morning, I remind my RPS that I am willing to face whatever fears immobilize me and listen to the guidance it provides. It is by no coincidence that help from people and programs begins appearing within a week.

A good friend, Kim Craft, who is an exceptional muscle and connective tissue (fascia) licensed Bowen therapist, finds significant muscle imbalances in my pelvis and upper body. Kim had begun doing muscle releases on my body weeks after the accident to stay ahead of contractures and help integrate the healing of all my muscle groups.

At the start of the New Year, increased walking with crutches and a cane had created excruciating pain between my shoulder blades and in my neck. From a whole-body perspective, Kim senses something neurological may be happening and suggests I seek medical advice.

In early March, I connect with Dr. Suehun Ho, a UPMC Physical Medicine Rehab specialist whose examination rules out nerve damage from the C7 fracture. Dr. Ho feels the muscle spasms are due to weakened shoulder girdle muscles. She also suspects I may be experiencing PTSD symptoms, along with latent vestibular dysfunction, from a concussion. She prescribes vestibular and upper body physical therapy and refers me to Alicia Puskar, Psy.D., a neuropsychologist at the UPMC Sports Medicine Concussion Program.

By early May 2017, Drs. Ho and Puskar, Kim, and PT's are helping me directly address the physical problems co-existing with my driving anxiety. Yet, the fear of other drivers at intersections still has a hard grip on me.

Dr. Puskar suggests I see a psychotherapist who deals with trauma and PTSD. Later in May, I find Nancy Mramor, Ph.D., an integrative psychotherapist who specializes in a mind/body/spirit approach to wellness and personal growth.

Dr. Mramor explains clearly how a traumatic accident such as mine can manifest differently in the body, compared to the mind and spirit. Through Nancy's help, I begin to understand that the cumulative trauma I've been experiencing goes beyond the physical trauma I have focused on exclusively. She helps me see that if I confront the emotional trauma, my body will positively respond and lessen its physical reactions.

When I am ready, Dr. Mramor guides me through the next steps of releasing the emotional trauma. Using her specialized training in Neuro Emotional Technique (NET), a kinesiology-based treatment along with hypnosis and Eye Movement Desensitization and Reprocessing (EMDR), Dr. Mramor enables me to literally "delete" the emotional source of my driving anxiety. She explains, "It is similar to deleting unwanted software from your computer."

For the next few months, I slowly build trust in Dr. Mramor's treatment by practicing "perfectly" the affirmations we create together, and, over time, my anxiety noticeably lessens.

Still, I feel the only way to truly know if I have deleted the fear of other drivers is to drive through the intersection where my accident occurred. In the months since I began driving again, I have driven near the intersection and on Forbes in the direction of the driver who hit me—but never through that intersection from the Jumonville Street side.

Why not drive through the intersection on the one-year anniversary of your accident? I ask myself. *This will certainly test if you have healed your body, mind, and spirit of the trauma.*

TRUE GRIT TEST

The morning of September 13, 2017, I depart from home at 8 a.m. to leave enough time to position myself on Jumonville Street for the 8:35 a.m. reenactment.

The morning has a strangely hazy, humid feel, similar to the same day last year. The memory sends goosebumps down my spine. I turn onto Jumonville at 8:20 a.m. and by chance find one empty parking spot near the Forbes intersection. The goosebumps continue as I sense from these "coincidences" that there is something meaningful about to happen.

While I wait, I watch cars, buses, and trucks go through multiple light cycles, taking note of their driving patterns and speeds. My observations cause me to reflect on how different I am today from how I was last year at this intersection.

A year ago at this exact light, I didn't notice the potted geraniums on the neighbor's stoop or the children and people gathered at the bus stop. My priorities were focused on getting to work to make money and build a business. I had been traveling in the same direction for years. Interestingly, following the impact when my car came to a stop after ricocheting off the rowhouse wall, it was facing opposite Jumonville in a *new* direction. I don't think that was by chance.

(Looking at the time) *Eight minutes to go.*

I feel different in other ways too. It isn't the unsightly surgical scars or the passing of an entire year of rehabilitation that makes me feel different. It's what I have done that makes me know that I *am* different. I survived a near-fatal accident, endured multiple surgeries, weathered complications and setbacks, and now I am doing what I promised myself I would do. I am walking, running, hiking, and playing basketball just as I did before the accident.

A year ago in ICU, I questioned if my life's purpose could be connected to this accident. Well, today I am certain of that purpose. Through the worst experience that ever happened to me, I discovered how to become well again by making positive choices.

I chose to embrace the power I have as the driver of this recovery. I chose to keep my eyes fixed on the vision of how well I wanted to be. I chose to accept help from family and friends, and I chose to use assistive devices that would help me regain my independence. I used my internal guidance system to rebound from setbacks. And most of all, I am here today to be defined by how I respond to the fear of this intersection.

These choices were deliberate decisions I made because I wanted so badly to become well again. I now know that getting well did not happen as a miracle or by chance. It happened as a result of what I envisioned and the inspired action I took. This rebounding journey also makes me certain of something else. I know I will use my accident experience to inspire, guide, and teach others how they too can choose to rebound deliberately from their own traumas.

Now, all that stands between me and knowing I can truly live my life with this new purpose is to drive through the intersection.

8:33 A.M. THE TRAFFIC LIGHT ON JUMONVILLE TURNS RED.

Swallowing hard, I slowly pull out of my parking space to become the lead car at the traffic light. As seconds tick and vehicles fly down Forbes Avenue, I breathe deeply, grip my steering wheel at ten and two o'clock…and wait.

8:35 A.M. THE LIGHT TURNS GREEN.

"Ready, Paula?" I say to myself. My heart is racing, beads of perspiration collect on my brow, and my grip tightens. I look up Forbes Avenue. I look again. I look a third time before stepping on the gas pedal.

The car slowly moves forward and while still taking glances up Forbes I say aloud, "I am the driver. I'm the planner and designer of my recovery. I am the person who got me to where I am today."

Just beyond the exact spot where my life was suddenly and unexpectedly redirected, I burst into tears and proclaim, "And now, I have chosen to be defined by how I overcame my fears!"

I pull over to park, and while I breathe deeply to calm down and let my heart rate slow, something becomes luminously clear, as though I am waking up from a dream.

I understand now what actually happened throughout this recovery journey.

A short distance from where I am now, I encountered, through the accident, the opportunity to test my intention to find the good in a bad situation. I had to go through all these months of up and down experiences in order to know what I value most in life. At the time I didn't understand what these challenges were suggesting or where they were leading. Yet, I never gave up believing I would find what I was looking for until I finally returned to where I am right now.

I am back where I belong!

Yes, I am home again in a body that is well. This life-changing journey *did* have an inspired purpose. It was meant to awaken in me a renewed respect and appreciation for being able to move, and breathe, and be the healthy person I am.

The immense joy and happiness I am experiencing right now feels mystically familiar. Why, of course, these are the exact feelings I experienced when I thought I died while in my personal Land of Oz. Like Dorothy's awakening, my awakening assures me that the power I needed to return to the health I wanted was always within me. I just needed the opportunity to find it.

Indisputably, I too can embrace the exuberant joy Dorothy felt upon seeing Aunty Em and realizing she and Toto were back in Kansas. Dorothy, I say it wholeheartedly with you now, "There *is* no place like home!"

Principle 6
Face Your Fears

As recovery involves the unknown, you will consistently face fears. These are not a sign of weakness but of being human. Rather than deny or run from your fears, face them and get the help you need to reach your goal.

EPILOGUE

I WISH I COULD SAY THAT AFTER DRIVING through the Jumonville intersection I lived happily ever after, but that would be facetious. Within a week of the one-year anniversary reenactment drive, another accident-related setback appeared.

It actually started around late August 2017, when I experienced a sharp pain in my chest while swimming. Subsequently, I began having shortness of breath with almost any activity, including lying down.

I was fortunate to be referred by a medical doctor friend to Dr. David O. Wilson, a critical care pulmonologist at UPMC. After a series of pulmonary tests, X-rays, and a CT scan, Dr. Wilson discovered a protruding diaphragm hernia in the same section that was injured in the accident. The laxity was allowing my stomach to migrate up into my lung cavity and not allowing my left lung to fully inflate. This was causing the shortness of breath.

After even more tests, on December 13, 2017, Dr. Inderpal Sarkaria, an internationally recognized thoracic surgeon at UPMC, performed a minimally invasive robotic plication repair of my diaphragm. Dr. Sarkaria literally sewed pleats into my diaphragm to tighten the laxity and allow my diaphragm to fully contract and expand my left lung. A 12-week recovery was necessary to allow enough scarring to strengthen the pleats and avoid a future hernia.

Hearing the news of a diaphragm injury was disappointing. However, with the validation from the reenactment fresh in my memory, I quickly saw this new surgery as yet another opportunity to apply the rebounding principles I had discovered from my recovery journey.

Instead of being engaged in the learning process during the recovery, with this surgery I could apply the principles from the start. And this is exactly what I did. My practiced skills of envisioning the outcome I wanted and taking inspired actions enabled me to make *yet another* remarkable recovery in record time.

I went into my surgery with a positive outcome statement that I recited daily to keep me focused and to drive my recovery. I prepared checklists and thought through all the many things I would need to thoroughly prepare myself for a successful surgery.

During the rehab period, I developed tracking systems to chart the progress I made with the breathing exercises I practiced "perfectly" each day. And once Dr. Sarkaria released me from his medical care, I created a progressive exercise plan to help me regain my aerobic fitness and strength.

I not only healed without complications, but I was also able to play in a Senior Olympic qualifying basketball tournament in April—four months after surgery. Drs. Sarkaria, Moloney, Wilson, and Ho were all surprised and pleased by my ability to not only heal properly but to quickly regain the state of health and fitness I desired.

MAKING LEMONADE FROM LEMONS

During the latter months of my accident recovery, when I saw the rebound I was making, I could feel the inkling of an entrepreneurial idea starting to germinate. Why not share the insights and principles I discovered with others who want to rebound from an accident, injury, or related surgery?

I began researching what is available for patients facing surgery, who are in rehab, or who have been released from medical care. I also talked with health professionals about the need for recovery mindset training. I learned one of the biggest frustrations medical practitioners experience when working with patients is the person's mindset that healthcare is "supposed to make them well."

Medical professionals clearly understand their role is to help a patient's body heal—and that the ownership for reaching wellness belongs to the patient. Yet, the problem is that most patients don't know how to work strategically with their healthcare team to heal and get well when facing a recovery situation.

The reasons for this lack of strategic cooperation are many. Most people aren't aware of what their wellbeing mindset is or how it is directing their current state of health and wellbeing. They may never have been shown how to embrace the power already within them or how to drive their healing to higher-than-expected levels. When patients don't know how to drive a recovery, they unknowingly let the power to get well go dormant. They then accept whatever level of healing they attain as "the best it can be"—when that state may be far below their potential.

The most unfortunate part is the disappointment and limitations patients experience when the healing outcomes are not what they expected. They question whether they made the right decisions. Some want to place blame on their doctor or the healthcare team for not making them well. This type of disappointment in outcomes does not have to be the norm.

I thought long and hard about the principles I used in my recovery. And I came to the conclusion that taking ownership of one's health and wellbeing can be learned—and the learning doesn't have to be difficult.

I began speaking to all levels of health practitioners about my idea of creating a simple process for patients to create and use a healing and wellbeing recovery plan. Their response was overwhelmingly positive, saying they would love for their patients to approach a recovery using a constructive positive mindset. This inspired me to act on my idea. On February 9, 2018, the inkling for a simple driving force recovery process became an established business called, Rebound Planner, LLC.

I began with a vision to create a planner-type tool that guides people through easy, effective steps they can take to drive their injury recovery. I started using the planner concept with clients to discover which tools help them stay in the driver seat of their recovery. The more we experimented, the better the process became and the greater health and wellness people experienced.

It was electrifying to see other people take charge of getting well and the positive outcomes they attain in their recovery. Their excitement at being in control of getting well is contagious. Patients, family members, and health providers experience the difference in a recovery when a patient sits in the driver's seat and takes control of the steering wheel.

Each time I see another person take control of his or her recovery, I remember when I first realized the significance of my steering wheel experience. It is exhilarating for me to watch what is resulting from an accidental collision with the opportunity to learn the power to get well. My choice to take hold of the steering wheel has been the driving force behind the full and robust life I am now living. And I am convinced it can be the driving force for you as well. You just need to get behind the wheel and decide where you want to go.

FULL RECOVERY

July 2017: Hiking in Frick Park with my sister Nancy.

April 2018: Up for a layup against NOVA Triple Threat.

April 2018: 60+ Butler Pursuit PA Senior Olympic gold medal winners. Coach Bill Lahr; Janet Smeltz; Paula Franetti; Tina Bruns; Jane Leo; Nancy Graham. (Not pictured: Lisa Adamsky; and Peg Schwinge Schipper)

Paula's Six Principles

Principle 1
Embrace Your Power

While you must accept that your life and body now have a new reality, you still have the power to make choices and determine your own physical outcome. To rebound to the highest level possible, you must hold onto your power with all your determination. Although times of discouragement are inevitable, you always have the power to change.

Principle 2
Envision Your Positive Outcome

Your thoughts and mindset determine outcomes. The more you can imagine the positive outcome of your rebounding effort with all your senses firing, the more likely you will manifest exactly what you imagine.

PRINCIPLE 3
ACCEPT HELP TO BUILD INDEPENDENCE

Your healing depends upon accepting, rather than resisting the help of a supportive community while you work to regain independence as soon as possible.

PRINCIPLE 4
LEVERAGE ASSISTIVE DEVICES

Relying on assistive devices is a path to independence rather than an admission of disability. Don't hinder your recovery by resisting this type of support.

PRINCIPLE 5
EXPECT AND REBOUND FROM SETBACKS

Setbacks are an inevitable and natural part of recovery. Facing each setback with humility, self-reliance, and acceptance enables you to keep moving forward at a realistic pace.

PRINCIPLE 6
FACE YOUR FEARS

As recovery involves the unknown, you will consistently face fears. These are not a sign of weakness but of being human. Rather than deny or run from your fears, face them and get the help you need to reach your goal.

About the Author

A **DIEHARD** positive thinker, Paula Franetti, MS, CHC, CPT, seizes the opportunity to thrive no matter where she looks, even in the bleakest situations. Having literally started over after a devastating automobile accident at age 60, Paula knows first-hand the struggle involved in a full recovery from life-altering injures and multiple surgeries.

Paula is an inspirational speaker, health coach, and lifestyle assessment expert. With over 30 years of health and "lifestyle-smarts," Paula combines her vast knowledge and experience in rehabilitation, exercise, and behavioral lifestyle change to inspire people through the many complicated phases of rehabilitation and healthy living.

In addition to being a sought-after speaker, Paula is the founder of Rebound Planner, LLC, and creator of the Rebound Planner Series—downloadable recovery planners for achieving personal wellness outcomes in three areas: pre-surgery, rehab, and beyond medical release.

Paula is a certified health and behavioral change coach with advanced training in cardiac rehab exercise physiology, lifestyle and weight management, and personal training. Her background also includes:

- *Health Solutions Innovator*—Designer of a personalized lifestyle management platform which interprets data from metabolic and wearable technologies and provides sustainable disease prevention and/or chronic disease management.
- *Health and Fitness Consultant*—Expert resource for individuals and corporate wellness programs that included personal training, nutrition consulting, and stress management.
- *Prosthetic & Orthotic (O&P) Facility Co-owner*—Led an O&P organization with multiple branches servicing multiple counties in Pennsylvania.
- *Motivational Wellness Speaker*—Multiple appearances, including television, radio, written media, corporate, insurance, and university settings.

To contact Paula or book her to speak to your group:

Website .... https://www.ReboundPlanner.com/

Email .... paula@ReboundPlanner.com

LinkedIn .... https://www.linkedin.com/in/paula-franetti/

Blog .... https://www.reboundplanner.com/blog/

Facebook .... https://www.facebook.com/ReboundPlanner/

Twitter .... https://twitter.com/ReboundP

Resources for You

Rebound Planners are your personal guidance system for regaining the health and wellbeing you want when recovering from an injury, accident or, related surgery. By deliberately planning from the start of whatever phase of recovery you are in, you stay in control and can lead your body to levels of wellbeing that reach beyond general healing.

Whether you are the one injured, a concerned loved one, or friend of someone who is, there are three planners to help regain the health and wellbeing everyone wants.

SURGERY REHAB BEYOND RELEASE

Each Planner in Our 3-Rebound Planner Series Contains:

- Positive outcome goal setting
- Worksheets, cheat sheets, to-do lists
- Checklists, timeline charts, schedulers
- Tracking systems for medications, pain, exercise, sleep, etc.
- Valuable tips on nutrition, stress management, exercise, etc.
- Certificate for two personalized coaching sessions with a certified health coach

Rebound Planners come in a downloadable format that gives you multiple options for easy use of your planner whether you are seeing your doctor, physical therapist, or other health provider.

Made in the USA
Coppell, TX
26 November 2019